"Archbishop Michael Fitzg[...] prayerful reflections on the [...] Qur'anic verses and followe[...] to mind as the mediation u[...] [...] arrangement generates a rich interplay between living sacred texts through eight developing themes. Throughout, he draws adeptly from decades of experience in Christian-Muslim studies and dialogue. *Praise the Name of the Lord* is a study guide for Christian-Muslim spiritual encounter, a scholarly contribution on two faiths in dialogue, and a prayerbook for remembering God."

> — John Borelli
> Georgetown University

"This beautiful reflection is valuable for anyone who wants to understand the Muslim tradition of meditation on God's Ninety-Nine Names more deeply. Archbishop Fitzgerald draws biblical and qur'anic passages into conversation with each other in a way that is accessible to everyone. An inspiring example of true dialogue of religious experience."

> — Sandra Toenies Keating
> Associate Professor of Theology
> Providence College

"Both Christians and Muslims recognize a God who creates, who draws near, who judges, and who guides. Both Muslims and Christians have also found many ways to name the aspects and attributes of the divine being. In this innovative book Archbishop Fitzgerald offers an insightful exploration of divine names drawn from both the Bible and the Qur'an, producing a volume that combines a fascinating excursus in comparative theology with a compendium of passages that can serve as material for a group retreat or for personal reflection."

> — Jane McAuliffe, PhD
> Director of National and International Outreach
> Library of Congress

"In this little volume, Archbishop Fitzgerald's meditations bear the mark of one who has studied deeply and with great integrity over a lifetime the sacred texts and languages of the Abrahamic faiths. Without compromising in the least his faithfulness to the Christian tradition, he deftly manages to present Muslim and Jewish renderings of the Names of God with the respect and objectivity reflective of his long years spent in dialogue with these communities. Importantly, while learned readers will surely benefit from his erudition, those currently laboring away at interreligious dialogue will also find themselves to be fortunate recipients of a wonderful model for *doing* intertextual studies of sacred texts."

> — Dr. Anthony Cirelli
> Associate Director
> Secretariat for Ecumenical and Interreligious Affairs
> United States Conference of Catholic Bishops

"Archbishop Michael Fitzgerald has devoted his life to the study of Islam and dialogue with Muslims. In *Praise the Name of the Lord* he skillfully combines scholarship and spiritual insight to show how the Islamic tradition of constant remembrance (*dhikr*) of the Beautiful Names of God can be a source of inspiration for Christians. As is the case for both Muslims and Christians, remembrance—*anamnesis* is the term in the Christian Scriptures—is meant to lead to praise of God and imitation of the divine qualities. Drawing on passages of the Holy Bible that resonate with various Names of God in the Nobel Qur'an, Archbishop Fitzgerald encourages readers, be they Christian or Muslim, to appreciate the spiritual riches of another religious tradition and to come to a deeper understanding and appreciation of their own."

> — William Skudlarek, OSB
> Secretary General, Monastic Interreligious Dialogue

Praise the Name of the Lord

Meditations on the Names of God
in the Qur'an and the Bible

Archbishop Michael Louis Fitzgerald, MAfr

Foreword by
Mary Margaret Funk, OSB

Afterword by
Zeki Saritoprak

LITURGICAL PRESS
Collegeville, Minnesota

www.litpress.org

This work was originally published as *Praise the Name of the Lord: Meditations on the Most Beautiful Names of God*, Collection Studi arabo-islamici del PISAI, no. 20 (Rome: Pontificio Instituto di Studi Arabi e d'Islamistica, 2015). Used by permission of PISAI.

Cover design by Monica Bokinskie. Image courtesy of Wikimedia Commons. This hilye, mounted on a wooden board, is unusual in having two side panels, similar to a Christian triptych. The central panel displays a textual description of the Prophet Muhammad. The side panels list the 99 names of God.

1   2   3   4   5   6   7   8   9

Library of Congress Cataloging-in-Publication Data

Names: Fitzgerald, Michael, 1937– author.
Title: Praise the name of the Lord : meditations on the names of God in the
    Qur'an and the Bible / Archbishop Michael Louis Fitzgerald.
Description: Collegeville, Minnesota : Liturgical Press, 2017. | Includes
    bibliographical references.
Identifiers: LCCN 2016043850 (print) | LCCN 2016051566 (ebook) (print) |
    LCCN 2016051566 (ebook) | ISBN 9780814645727 | ISBN 9780814645987
    (ebook)
Subjects: LCSH: God—Name. | God (Christianity)—Name. | God (Islam)—Name.
Classification: LCC BL473 .F58 2017 (print) | LCC BL473 (ebook) | DDC
    231—dc23
LC record available at https://lccn.loc.gov/2016043850

This publication is dedicated to all, whether men or women, of whatever religion or of none, in all parts of the world, who are endeavoring to increase mutual understanding and to strengthen cooperation between Christians and Muslims.

Contents

Acknowledgements

In the first place I would like to express my gratitude to the superiors of the Society of Missionaries of Africa, the Society to which I have the privilege and joy of belonging, for having given me the opportunity of studying theology in Carthage, Tunisia, where I was also able to begin the study of Arabic. Later, the same superiors allowed me to continue these studies at the Pontifical Gregorian Institute in Rome and at the School of Oriental and African Studies in London. I wish to thank my colleagues and also the students at the Pontifical Institute of Arabic and Islamic Studies in Rome for their inspiration, and in particular the late Father Robert Caspar, who, by communicating his knowledge, but also by his example, encouraged me to take an open and positive attitude toward the Qur'an.

I would like to thank the different groups of priests and religious women who, over the years, have followed the meditations presented in this book. Their interest for these spiritual exercises has motivated me to prepare them for publication and so present them to a wider public.

I owe much to the confidence that has been shown to me by two Muslim colleagues, Said Hamdun, at the University of

Makerere, Kampala, Uganda, and Zeki Saritoprak, at John Carroll University, University Heights, Ohio, USA, who graciously accepted to write the afterword for this book. May they accept the expression of my gratitude.

My thanks go also to the authorities of John Carroll University who, within the framework of the Tuohy Chair for Interreligious Studies, have given me the freedom and time to prepare the manuscript for publication. An adapted version of the introduction and the meditations provided the matter for the Tuohy Lectures of 2015. I wish to thank also the staff of the Graselli Library of this university for their constantly kind cooperation.

The meditations presented here were originally written in French, and my thanks go to Sr. Thérèse Grasland, SCSL, for her comments and corrections, which greatly helped to improve the texts. The translation into English is my own work, so I am entirely responsible for any infelicities.

I am grateful to Mary Margaret Funk, OSB, who readily agreed to write the preface to this English edition of my book.

Abbreviations

ABD	*The Anchor Bible Dictionary*
CBC	*Collegeville Bible Commentary*
EI²	*Encyclopaedia of Islam*, 2ème édition.
EQ	*The Encyclopedia of the Qur'an*
JB	*The Jerusalem Bible*
MIDEO	*Mélanges de l'Institut Dominicain d'Etudes Orientales*
NRSV	*The New Revised Standard Version* (of the Bible)
NT	New Testament
OT	Old Testament
PISAI	Pontificio Istituto di Studi Arabi e d'Islamistica
Q	Qur'an; quotations from the Qur'an are indicated in the following way: Q 1:7, indicates *sûra* (chapter) 1, verse 7.
TOB	*La Traduction Oecuménique de la Bible*

Foreword

Archbishop Michael L. Fitzgerald's *Praise the Name of the Lord: Meditations on the Names of God in the Qur'an and the Bible* invites readers to encounter God through Muslim and Christian sacred texts. Some believe that the Mystery is the same fire deep inside, like a volcano, and we'll discover that all religions are really One. Brother David Steindl-Rast holds this view. Father William Skudlarek, OSB, from his experience in Buddhist/Catholic monastic dialogue observes that there's much in common in the day-to-day contemplative practices for monks and nuns but we might be heading toward different "destinations" (i.e., "karma" and "heaven" are very different).

If I reflect on my years in monastic dialogue I wonder if we are closer to a shared insight when gently grasped by "not-knowing." Perhaps we just don't know "if we are all one" or "if we differ." Archbishop Michael Fitzgerald in this book gifts us with a way of praying together without any agenda that the "other" see and do it "our" way. This book is a method for individuals and groups to see "the other" from the inside. This promotes understanding and deep appreciation.

I met Archbishop Michael in Rome when he was working at the Pontifical Council for Interreligious Dialogue. He not only received our reports and facilitated us to engage in dialogue with other Vatican officers but also joined us at gatherings in Assisi, Chicago, Louisville, and other conferences. Once I lamented to him about statements from the Vatican, such as *Dominus Ieusus*, which I felt were pushing back on insights gained at Vatican II. He deflected my concerns: "I'm working on a manuscript about the ninety-nine Names of God and some parallel passages from our Christian Bible." He then went on to share that this sustained *lectio* was inspiring his own prayer, his preparation for various homilies, lectures, writings, and participation at interfaith meetings.

So, when I read this manuscript in 2016, I paused. I could imagine Archbishop Michael praying over the Names of God. He had preached this retreat to some of his confreres in Algeria, before the civil conflict that was to bring about the deaths of four of them in Tizi-Ouzou and the drama of the captivity and killing of the seven Trappist monks of Notre Dame de l'Atlas, Tibhirine. Could such meditations still be presented? Would they need to be changed? The same question would arise later, when Archbishop Michael was nuncio in Cairo during the Arab Spring. While I was safe and sound in the cozy cloister of Glencairn Abbey, Ireland, writing a book on sustained *lectio*, he was doing it, and doing *lectio* as a Catholic bishop in a Muslim culture. I was writing in my "English language only" strong suit while he was drilling down deeply into these ancient texts using his knowledge of Arabic and writing both in French and in English. He could, of course, be encouraged by the example of Christian de Chergé, the prior of the Trappists of Tibhirine, who even in the face of death maintained an openness to the spiritual message of Islam.

Even though the method Archbishop Michael uses is Ignatian and not my usual way of doing monastic *lectio*, I took a week for a retreat "in place" and did what he suggested in the book. He clustered the texts in eight themes: God the Creator; The Transcendent God; God with Us; The God of Goodness and Mercy; God, Lord and King; God the Guide; The God Who Is Generous and Faithful; God, Our Peace. He provided a reflection on Moses and the Burning Bush that gave me a taste. The God who reveals Himself to us using Q 20:8-14; 1:6; 20:24 echo's the Christian Scripture's Exodus 3:1-7, 9-14; Isaiah 1:3-18; and Luke 1:38, which cites the Christian story of Moses, Samuel, and Mary.

I selected the name of God used in the first chapter, "God the Creator." I meditated on the eighteen passages from the Qur'an, the sixteen passages from the Old Testament, and the five passages from the New Testament. Therefore, I simply did *lectio* on the texts provided by Archbishop Michael's book.

When I paused and reflected on the citations from the Qur'an, I heeded the admonition that reading these texts will demand an effort; it will require that time be set aside for the purpose. It could be said that, like Moses, the reader has to make a detour. Meditating on the Names of God also demands a certain degree of purification, for one is approaching a holy place; one is coming nearer to God. One has to accept to remain in the place, even if at times it seems rather like a desert. Shoes or sandals have to be taken off, as a sign of respect, but also as a sign of the desire to remain in the presence of the Lord since, barefoot, one is not really ready to leave (p. xxx).

We can recognize that the Bible and the Qur'an are both part of the heritage of humanity as we seek to live together in peace and mutual understanding. We are well served to discover the Qur'an from within. I had never done a personal retreat using texts from the Qur'an and continued on with my own Christian Scriptures. In fact, this was the first time I had done a retreat on the theme of "my Creator God." There was a sweet harmony. My Catholic tradition is hinged on the name of creature claiming our Creator. Moral surges of courage and purpose cleansed my rusty soul. The prayer to that Creator God rose unbidden. The daily chanting of the psalms became brand-new, once again. Audaciously, it seems that while we have so many names for God maybe any and/or all of them lifts us in Prayer of Praise. Maybe the actual litany of all the names are God speaking to God while the creature, without shoes, kneels in adoration.

This book takes the reader steep and deep. When the United States invaded Iraq in 2004, I authored a book on Islam through Lantern Press. In my years as a catechist I felt we Catholics knew so little about Muslims and the tradition of Islam. Now, some years later, I feel that we have met devout Muslims and have some feel for Islam, including [the Holy] its Prophet Muhammad, but we have much work to do to "feel" from the inside our distinctive yet revealed experience of God.

Mary Margaret Funk, OSB
Our Lady of Grace
Beech Grove, Indiana

Introduction

The Most Excellent Names belong to God: use them to call on Him. (Q 7:180)[1]

The best names belong to Him.
Everything in the heavens and earth glorifies Him. (Q 59:24)

These verses from the Qur'an can be compared with what is said in Ps 113 [112]:

Praise the Lord!
Praise, O servants of the Lord;
    praise the name of the Lord.
Blessed be the name of the Lord
    from this time on and forevermore.
From the rising of the sun to its setting
the name of the Lord is to be praised. (Ps 113 [112]:1-3)[2]

---

[1] Quotations from the Qur'an, unless otherwise stated, will be made following the translation of M.A.S. Abdel Haleem, *The Qur'an* (Oxford: Oxford University Press, 2010).

[2] Quotations from the Bible, unless otherwise stated, will be made according to the New Revised Standard Version (NRSV).

The divine Names act at the same time as a *bridge* and an *invitation*. They act as a *bridge* in so far as they establish communication between God and human beings. God expresses Himself through His Names: through them we can go to Him.

These Names also constitute an *invitation*, first of all to praise: call on Him; celebrate His praises; praise the Name of the Lord. They also invite to imitation. Islamic tradition speaks of *al-takhalluq bi-akhlâq Allâh*, to clothe oneself with the habits of God, or with the divine attributes. The invitation is to contemplate the Names of God, so that if God is Just, we also should be just; if God is Merciful, then we too should show mercy; if God is Faithful, then faithfulness is our duty also. In the Gospel we find a similar invitation, or, rather, a command: "Be merciful, just as your Father is merciful" (Luke 6:36).

It seems appropriate here to quote a Muslim author, Abdennour Bidar, though without necessarily agreeing with his fundamental thesis concerning the radical autonomy of the human person in relation to God.

> Let us remember here that the God of the Qur'an has Himself precisely defined that which forms his own "flesh" through enumerating throughout the Qur'an a series of ninety-nine Names, each one more remarkable than the other. . . This is probably why the Qur'an in fact ceaselessly exhorts human beings to adopt an exclusive orientation and to meditate constantly and repeatedly on these Names, while on the contrary it repudiates anything which could turn them away from this contemplation: associating something with God, impiety, hypocrisy, unbelief, etc. The Qur'an is constantly directing the gaze of human beings towards these perfect qualities and infinite capacities because it wishes to let it be understood that human beings have been made in order

to appropriate them for themselves. The final aim of meditation on the divine Names is *to intensify their presence in ourselves,* to develop progressively, generation after generation, their activity, their strength and the fullness in ourselves.[3]

Christian readers may perhaps ask about the reason for the undertaking that lies at the basis of the present book, namely, to adopt as the point of departure for a series of meditations the texts of another religion. Muslim readers, likewise, may wonder how the texts of the Bible, whether of the Old Testament or of the New Testament, concern them. The idea behind this venture is to encourage dialogue with the persons among whom we are living. It is quite common now to speak of four kinds of inter-religious dialogue: the dialogue of life, the dialogue of action, the dialogue of formal exchanges, and the dialogue of religious experience. This last form of dialogue has been described in the following way: "[a dialogue] where persons, rooted in their own religious traditions, share their spiritual riches, for instance with regard to prayer and contemplation, faith and ways of searching for God or the Absolute."[4] Here, in this book, there is obviously no direct encounter of persons belonging to different traditions, more precisely between Christians and Muslims, but only an

[3] Abdennour Bidar, *L'islam sans soumission. Pour un existentialisme musulman* (Paris: Albin Michel, 2008), pp. 158–59, emphasis in the original.

[4] Pontifical Council for Interreligious Dialogue and the Congregation for the Evangelization of Peoples, *Dialogue and Proclamation*, 1991, no. 42; see Francesco Gioia, *Interreligious Dialogue: The Official Teaching of the Catholic Church from the Second Vatican Council to John Paul II (1963–2005)* (Boston: Pauline Books & Media, 2006), no. 966.

offering of texts that come from the sources of their respective spiritualities.

In this context I would like to recall something written by Father Jean-Muhammad Abd el-Jalîl, a Muslim who became a Christian and subsequently a Franciscan friar: "Certainly one of the best ways of understanding a people is to meditate on the texts they use for prayer."[5] To pray by starting from the texts of another religion can therefore help us to acquire a better appreciation of that religion. Its riches can be discovered. It may be that what we discover is not essential for the practice of our own religion, but it is possible that we will find different echoes that can capture our attention and may nourish our prayer.

This is a venture that has been undertaken by a group of Christians living in Algeria, men and women who for the most part are members of different religious congregations. Having come to realize that constant reference to Islamic spirituality could help them to live their respective vocations in the midst of Muslims, they formed an association that they called *Ribâṭ al-salâm* (the Bond of Peace). They would select a topic that each one was to investigate personally in the Qur'an and other Islamic sources, as well as in the Bible, and then they would come together, once or twice a year, to share their discoveries. The following are some of the topics they covered: "Do justice and walk humbly with your God"; "Living in an attitude of thanksgiving"; "Compassion—the language of the heart"; "Hospitality as a fruit of compassion." Their example has greatly encouraged me to continue this re-

[5] Jean-Mohammed Abd El-Jalîl, *Aspects intérieurs de l'Islam* (Paris: Le Seuil, 1949), p. 117.

flection on the Beautiful Names of God according to the Islamic tradition and their meaning for Christians.

There is, nevertheless, a double pitfall to be avoided. On the one hand, care must be taken not to give a false interpretation to the meaning of the sacred books of other religions. An effort has been made here to avoid a Christian reading of the Qur'an that would try to eliminate all the differences. The texts are to be allowed to speak for themselves. At the same time, it is necessary to remain faithful to one's own tradition. That is why, in the meditations proposed here, the presentation of texts from the Qur'an is followed by texts from the Bible, both from the Old Testament, or First Testament, as it might be better termed, and from the New Testament. The hope is that the parallel presentation of these texts may touch both mind and heart.

Is it permissible to take inspiration from the texts of another religion? In answer to this question I would like to quote another text, this time taken from the charter of the Groupe de Recherche Islamo-Chrétien (GRIC), the Muslim-Christian Research Group, a body of French-speaking Christians and Muslims who have been meeting and studying together since 1977.

> We do not think that the divine Word, the foundation of our faith, belongs exclusively to us, whether we be Christians or Muslims. Christian faith is based on the person of Jesus and the witness of the Apostles' faith as contained in the New Testament. But the historical phenomenon of Jesus of Nazareth, and the texts of the New Testament writings, are facts and documents available for investigation by all. Similarly Islamic faith is based on the Qur'an and the authentic tradition of the Prophet. But the qur'anic text and the life of Muhammad b. Abdallah form part of the general history of the human race and belong to its spiritual heritage.

This is why on both sides, with regard to the historical facts that ground our faith and with regard to our scriptures, we accept "readings" other than our own.[6]

These "readings" may provide us with a different understanding of the same term, of the same divine Name, since the resonances may vary according to the creed of each one. Here we can learn from the wisdom of an Anglican bishop, Kenneth Cragg, who has written:

Words in prayer, within or beyond our faith-community, are never more than the opportunity of the soul, the voice of our intention. Truly we must care for them scrupulously. But it is we who give them their reality and they must be seen as spaces and not as prisons for our hearts. . .

There is always the possibility that an agreement on terms, even with a difference with regard to their connotations, but with sincerity of heart, may grow and end up finally with a greater consensus.[7]

The consensus may lead to communion, a communion beyond words, in shared silence.

It is not the aim of this book to provide a complete study of the Names of God. For that the reader could consult Ghazâlî's classical work on the subject or the book by Daniel Gimaret.[8] It

---

[6] Muslim-Christian Research Group, *The Challenge of the Scriptures: The Bible and the Qur'an* (Maryknoll, NY: Orbis Books, 1989), pp. 11–12.

[7] Kenneth Cragg, *Alive to God: Muslim and Christian Prayer* (Oxford: Oxford University Press, 1970), p. 21.

[8] al-Ghazâlî, *The Ninety-Nine Beautiful Names of God* (*al-maqṣad al-asnâ fî sharḥ asmâ' Allâh al-ḥusnâ*), trans. David B. Burrell and Nazih Daher (Cambridge, UK: Islamic Texts Society, 1992); Daniel Gimaret, *Les noms divins en*

may nevertheless be useful to say a few words about "this characteristic feature of Islamic religion, namely the eminent place which the divine Names occupy in it."[9]

According to tradition, there are ninety-nine Names of God. A *hadîth* encourages their recitation:

> To God belong the 99 Names, that is one hundred minus one, for He, the Unique (*al-witr*—literally "the odd"), loves to be designated by these Names, enumerated one by one; he who knows the 99 Names will enter Paradise.[10]

A rosary will often be used as a support for the recitation of these Names. The Muslim rosary, the *subḥa*, is made up of three times thirty-three grains, or often simply of thirty-three. Ninety-nine is obviously 100 minus 1, the one missing being the Supreme Name, or the Hidden Name, proof that the Names given to God in human language can never entirely encompass or exhaust the mystery of God. God will always remain "Greater," well beyond that which we can say of Him.

The ninety-nine Names that Islam gives traditionally to God are drawn from the Qur'an, either directly or, after having been

---

Islam (Paris: Editions du Cerf, 1988). See also EQ, s.v. "God and His Attributes"; Maurice Borrmans, "Les musulmans et les Beaux Noms d'Allâh," *La Vie Spirituelle* (May–June 1988): pp. 349–61; Christian Chessel, "Les noms divins, porche d'entrée à la théologie musulmane," *Se comprendre* 98, no. 1 (January 1993); Angelo Scarabel, *Preghiera sui Nomi più belli. I novantanove Nomi di Dio nella tradizione islamica* (Genoa: Marietti, 1996). Further details will be found in Zeki Saritoprak's afterword to the present volume.

[9] Gimaret, *Les noms divins*, p. 7.

[10] Text quoted by L. Gardet, EI², s.v. "Al-Asma' al-Husna"; see also EI², s.v. "Witr."

formed from qur'anic expressions, particularly from verbs. For example, the Qur'an says that God is endowed with knowledge; therefore He is *al-ʿalîm*, the One who Knows. It should be noted that the faithful Muslim is not authorized to invent Names for God. When a popular Egyptian writer, Mustafa Mahmûd, a medical doctor who wrote spiritual books, spoke of God as an Architect, this raised quite a hullabaloo. This restriction puts a limit to the number of possible Names for God.

In fact, however, many more than ninety-nine Names can be derived from the Qur'an. Ghazâlî includes in his study a short chapter "on explaining that the names of God most high are not limited to ninety-nine so far as divine instruction is concerned."[11] Moreover, since several lists of ninety-nine Names are to be found, and since not all the Names coincide, many more than ninety-nine exist in reality.[12] One scholar has calculated that there could be over 130.[13] The list used as a basis for the reflections presented here, reproduced in the appendix, was published in Arabic and French in the review of the Pontifical Institute of Arabic and Islamic Studies, *Etudes Arabes*.[14] The list in Arabic is represented in the form of a lamp (cf. Q 24:35). It would appear to be the list of Walîd b. Muslim al-Dimashqî (d. 195/810), which is held to go back to Abû Hurayra, a companion

[11] Cf. al-Ghazâlî, *The Ninety-Nine Beautiful Names*, pp. 167–69.

[12] A Shi'ite handbook contains a list of the Ninety-Nine Names, eleven of which are not found in the list that has formed the basis of my study; cf. *Know Your Islam*, 2nd ed. (Bombay: Anjuman-e-Himayatul Islam, 1970), pp. 23–26.

[13] Cf. Zeki Saritoprak, "God and His Most Beautiful Names as Presented by the Sufi Orders," in *Kopru*, 1995, pp. 80–92 (in Turkish).

[14] "Les 'Noms' divins," in *Etudes Arabes* 20, pp. 44–45.

of Muhammad, and is to be found in the collection of *ḥadîths* compiled by al-Tirmidhî (d. 279/892).[15]

The list ends with the following prayer:

> My God, indeed I am Your servant, the son of Your servant, the son of Your handmaid. My forelock is in Your hands: Your judgment concerning me is decisive and Your decree is just. I therefore beseech You, by each one of the Names that belongs to You, which You have chosen for Yourself, or which You have revealed in Your book, or which You have taught to one of Your creatures, or the usage of which You have reserved to Yourself according to the knowledge You have of Your own Mystery, to render the glorious Qur'an true nourishment for my heart and light for my vision; may it dispel in me all sadness and remove from me every worry and affliction. Amen!

It will not be possible to reflect on all the ninety-nine Names of God within the compass of this small book. I have selected some of them, grouping them according to the following plan of meditation.

1. The Creator who upholds His creation
2. The Transcendent God, God's inner being
3. The Immanent God, God-with-us
4. The God of Love and Pardon
5. The Almighty King
6. The God who guides
7. The Generous God
8. The God of Peace

---

[15] Cf. Gimaret, *Les noms divins*, pp. 55–56.

This choice has been made keeping in mind the general flow of the Spiritual Exercises of St. Ignatius of Loyola. I am fully aware that some important Names of God, such as *al-ḥaqq* (Truth, Reality) and *al-ʿadl* (the Just One), have not been considered, or have been mentioned only in passing. Each meditation begins by presenting some of the Names of God as found in the Qurʾan and then continues by looking at similar themes in the Bible, both in the OT and the NT.[16] In some cases this will lead to the discovery of different emphases and even of Names that do not occur in the Qurʾan, such as "Shepherd." At times the Names in the Qurʾan are considered in a somewhat isolated fashion, making abstraction of their context, which may contain statements that go against Christian beliefs. I hope that this will be excused. In fact, we act in a similar way with regard to the Psalms and other books of the OT when we leave out certain verses that clash with our Christian sensitivity.

One final observation. These texts are proposed not as an object of study but in order to lead to meditation and prayer.[17] When quoting from the Qurʾan, the Arabic is often given in transcription in a parallel column. This is so that the savor of the original language may be better appreciated. A restricted use will be made of learned considerations, based on philology or Arabic grammar, when these can help to illuminate the meaning of a particular text.

[16] On the Names of God in the Bible, see *The Anchor Bible Dictionary* (ABD), s.vv. "Names of God in the OT," "God, in the OT," and " God, in the NT. "

[17] The meditations that form the eight chapters of the book have already been proposed to groups of Christians in North Africa, in Jerusalem, and in Egypt. They have been reworked for this book. Some parts of this introduction and of the first two chapters have appeared in my article "The Most Beautiful Names of God: Their Meaning for a Christian," *Islamochristiana* 35 (2009) : pp. 15–30.

Let me immediately add a remark of this kind. One finds in the Qur'an that two Names are constantly linked together: *wa-aᶜlamû anna Llâha ghaniyyᵘⁿ ḥamîd*, "Remember that God is self-sufficient, worthy of all praise" (Q 2:267 and *passim*). The term *ghanî*, which in common parlance means "rich," is here correctly translated "self-sufficient." God is not in need of anything; He does not even need our praise. This may recall for Catholics the fourth common preface for the Eucharist in which we find these words: "You have no need of our praise, yet our desire to thank you is itself your gift. Our prayer of thanksgiving adds nothing to your greatness, but makes us grow in your grace." If we meditate on the Names of God, it is not in order to give pleasure to God, but because God has something to give us. The words of the *Fâtiḥa* come to mind:

It is You we worship;   *iyyâ-ka naᶜbudu*
It is You we ask for help.   *wa-iyyâ-ka nastaᶜîn*
   (Q 1:5)

And now, to end this introduction, an initial meditation on the God who reveals Himself to us.

God—there is no god but Him—the most excellent names belong to Him.

Has the story of Moses come to you [Prophet]? He saw a fire and said to his people, "Stay here, I can see a fire. Maybe I can bring you a flaming brand from it or find some guidance there." When he came to the fire, he was called: "Moses! I am your Lord. Take off your shoes: you are in the sacred valley of Ṭuwa.[18]

[18] Abdel Haleem gives no explanation for this name. Another translator of the Qur'an, Yusuf Ali, notes: "This was the valley just below Mount Sinai,

> I have chosen you, so listen to what is being revealed. I am God;
> there is no god but Me and keep up the prayer so that you re-
> member me. (Q 20:8-14)

Some remarks on this text. First of all we see that Moses is driven
by his curiosity—and curiosity, according to popular wisdom,
is the beginning of knowledge. He wants to find out the nature
of this fire. He accepts to be taken out of his way, to go out of
himself. He thinks of his family, for whom he might be able to
bring a flaming brand and so light a fire that could warm them
in the desert. He may also find the right direction (*hudâ*): in the
material sense, this might mean being told which way to go to
find water and a good camping place, but there is also a spiritual
sense, namely, to go in the right direction, along the straight path,
as indicated in the *Fâtiḥa*:

Guide us to the straight path.	*ihdinâ l-ṣirâṭ al-mustaqîm*
(Q 1:6)	

Having reached the fire, Moses receives a personal invitation. He
is addressed by his own name. The One who is speaking to him
establishes with him a personal relationship: "I am *your* Lord."

This meeting entails purification, for Moses finds himself in a
sacred place. He also discovers that he has been chosen by God
for a mission that will soon be entrusted to him (cf. Q 20:24),

---

where subsequently he [Moses] was to receive the Law. In the parallel mystic
meaning, we are selected by trials in this humble life, whose valley is just as
sacred and receives God's glory just as the heights of the Mount (*Ṭur*) if we but
have the insight to perceive it," *The Holy Qur'an* (Beirut: Dar al Arabia, 1968),
p. 792, n. 2544. It is possible that Ṭuwa might come from the Syriac *ṭur/ṭura*,
"the mountain"; cf. EQ, s.v. "*Ṭuwâ*."

but, before speaking, he must listen, and he must be careful to give worship exclusively to the one God.

Now let us consider the parallel text in the Bible.

> Moses was keeping the flock of his father-in-law Jethro, the priest of Midian; he led his flock beyond the wilderness, and came to Horeb, the mountain of God. There the angel of the Lord appeared to him in a flame of fire out of a bush; he looked, and the bush was blazing, yet it was not consumed. Then Moses said: "I must turn aside and look at this great sight, and see why the bush is not burned up." When the Lord saw that he had turned aside to see, God called to him out of the bush, "Moses, Moses!" And he said: "Here I am." Then he said: "Come no closer! Remove the sandals from your feet, for the place on which you are standing is holy ground." He said further: "I am the God of your father, the God of Abraham, the God of Isaac, and the God of Jacob." And Moses hid his face for he was afraid to look at God.
>
> Then the Lord said, "I have observed the misery of my people who are in Egypt; I have heard their cry on account of their taskmasters. Indeed I know their sufferings. . . . So come, I will send you to Pharaoh to bring my people, the Israelites, out of Egypt." But Moses said to God, "Who am I that I should go to Pharaoh, and bring the Israelites out of Egypt?" He said, "I will be with you; and this shall be the sign for you that it is I who sent you: when you have brought the people out of Egypt, you shall worship God on this mountain."
>
> But Moses said to God, "If I come to the Israelites and say to them, 'The God of your ancestors has sent me to you,' and they ask me, 'What is his name?' what shall I say to them?" God said to Moses, "I AM WHO I AM." He said further, "Thus you shall say to the Israelites, 'I AM has sent me to you.'" (Exod 3:1-7, 9-14)

We find here, as in the qur'anic text, the same curiosity on the part of Moses that leads him to make a detour; the invitation that is addressed to him; the purification that is required. Yet there are differences also: the event takes place at the mountain of God; the fire is not consumed; Moses answers God, saying "Here I am," which could remind us of the young Samuel (cf. 1 Sam 1:3-18), and also perhaps of Mary who, at the time of the Annunciation, pronounced her *fiat* to God's messenger, Gabriel (cf. Luke 1:38). God reveals Himself as the God who intervenes in history: in the past (he is God of the ancestors), in the present (he has seen the misery of His people), and in the future (he entrusts Moses with a mission). Moses is to accomplish this mission in the strength of the Lord, the strength of His Name: "I will be what I will be."

From these texts it is possible to draw some guidance that may help in the reading of the meditations that follow. Reading these texts will demand an effort; it will require that time be set aside for this purpose. It could be said that, like Moses, the reader has to make a detour. Meditating on the Names of God also demands a certain degree of purification, for one is approaching a holy place; one is coming nearer to God. One has to accept to remain in this place, even if at times it may seem rather like a desert. Shoes or sandals have to be taken off, as a sign of respect, but also as a sign of the desire to remain in the presence of the Lord, since, barefoot, one is not really ready to leave.

It is possible that, in the course of these meditations, God will address a personal invitation to the reader. In this case, one should be attentive to what the Lord is asking, to the mission that he is entrusting, a mission that goes beyond the person of the individual to those to whom he or she is being sent. It is by God's favor and grace that this mission is entrusted, and it is through the grace of God that it will be accomplished. The mystery of the burning bush includes the fire that does not consume, symbolizing energy that is never spent—the love of God. If we trust in our own energy, in our own limited human strength, we shall soon be exhausted, burnt out. We are called to empty ourselves in order to leave room for divine energy, the source of all goodness and well-being.

1
God the Creator

We can state quite roundly that for us everything starts with creation, or rather with the Creator God. We are invited to place ourselves before this God with thanksgiving in our hearts for all that He has done, and is doing, for us. At the same time we can be aware of a possible twofold reaction. On the one hand, we become conscious of our own weakness, of the fact that we are not the masters of our own existence. We realize that we are radically dependent on God. On the other hand, we can appreciate our own dignity, which is founded on the will of God to create us and on the role that he has entrusted to us in the midst of Creation.

1. *The Teaching of the Qur'an*

Among the ninety-nine Names of God there are several that refer to the Creator. We find three of them in one single passage:

> He is God: the Creator (*al-khâliq*), the Originator (*al-bâri'*), the Shaper (*al-muṣawwir*). (Q 59:24)

The last-mentioned Name indicates one who gives a shape, an image (*ṣûra*) to something.[1]

In *al-baqara,* the second *sûra*, there is found another Name:

> He is the Originator (*badîʿ*) of the heavens and the earth.
> (Q 2:117)

The verb used would suggest the production of something that is new, a new beginning (it may be remembered that the term *bidʿa* is used by Muslim jurists to refer to an innovation, something regarded as heretical).

This passage continues by giving an explanation of the way God proceeds:

> And when He decrees something, He says only "Be," and it is.
> (Q 2:117)

This verb is very close in form to another, *badaʾa*, which means "to begin." In one text in the Qur'an this verb is used within the context of creation:

---

[1] See Daniel Gimaret, *Les noms divins en Islam*, pp. 279–311. With regard to these three Names found in Q 59:24, the great theologian al-Ghazâlî (d. 505/1111) says that they are not synonymous, but rather correspond to three stages in the process of creation: God first conceives the project of creation, He is *al-khâliq*; next He brings into being as *al-bâriʾ*; and finally He gives shape to the new being as *al-muṣawwir* (cf. al-Ghazâlî, *The Ninety-Nine Beautiful Names*, pp. 68–72; see also Gimaret, *Les noms divins*, p. 282). Roger Arnaldez, however, remarks that it is useless to look for two different words in European languages to represent *khâliq* and *bâriʾ*, which are considered as synonyms. He notes that *al-khâliq*, with the article, is applied only to God; cf. EI2, s.v. "Khalḳ." Present in the Qur'an there is also the intensive form *al-khallâq* (Q 1:86; 36:81), which would signify that God never ceases to create. See also EQ, s.v. "God and His Attributes," pp. 326–27.

> It is He who created [you] in the first place (*yabda'u*), and He will
> do so again, so that He may justly reward those who believe and
> who do good deeds. (Q 10:4)

We see from this text that the Creator God is also Judge. He has
created, but He can also repeat this act of creation or, in other
words, he can make creation return to Him for judgment, just
as the desert, which may seem dead, can come to life once rain
has fallen. In fact, in the Qur'an creation is seen as a sign of the
power of God, who is able to bring human beings to life again at
the end of time so that they may undergo judgment.

I would like to mention here a Name that is not found in
al-Tirmidhî's list, *al-fâṭir,* "the Creator,"[2] but that occurs in the
Qur'an, precisely in *sûrat al-fâṭir*, Q 35:

> Praise be to God, Creator (*fâṭir*) of the heavens and earth. . . .
> He adds to creation as He will. (Q 35:1)

It would seem that the root FṬR means "separate," thus suggesting
here that creation is carried out by separating, or distinguishing,
the heavens from the earth. This Name *al-fâṭir* occurs in another
place, this time in connection with judgment:

> Say, "God! Creator (*fâṭir*) of the heavens and earth! Knower of all
> that is hidden and all that is open, You will judge between your
> servants regarding their differences." (Q 39:46)

Just as in creation the different elements are separated one from
the other, so also judgment will take the form of separation between the just and the wicked.

---

[2] Cf. Gimaret, *Les noms divins*, pp. 290–91. Al-Ghazâlî does not discuss
this Name.

There are two things that become apparent from these texts: the first is that in creating God is absolutely free, and second, that creation remains a mystery. This is very different from the theory of emanation according to which all things develop from God by necessity, a theory prominent in Gnostic thought and found in the writings of some Muslim philosophers.

The question can, in fact, be asked: why has God created, He who is *al-qayyûm*, the Self-Subsistent, *al-ghanî,* the Rich, the one who has no need of anything? Does not the answer to this question belong to *al-ghayb*, that which is hidden, the Mystery? It is worth underlining this, since Islam is often presented as the rational religion par excellence, yet here we come face to face with a mystery that is at the very foundation of our existence.

This mystery brings forth a cry of astonishment and arouses an attitude of thanksgiving toward the Creator:

> Read! In the name of your Lord who created: He created man from a clinging form. (Q 96:1-2)[3]

This forms part of the initial message of Islam. These verses have been recognized both by traditional Islamic scholars and by Orientalists as belonging to the first passage of the Qur'an considered chronologically. The verses arouse grateful recognition on the part of human beings:

> People, remember God's grace towards you. Is there any creator (*khâliq*) other than God to give you sustenance from the heavens

---

[3] Yusuf Ali translates: "Proclaim! (or Read!) In the name of thy Lord and Cherisher who created—Created man out of a (mere) clot of congealed blood."

and earth? There is no God but Him. How can you be so deluded?
(Q 35:3)

To wish not to recognize the Creator, to refuse one's dependence on Him, constitutes *kufr*, which is the cardinal sin of ingratitude and disbelief. From the purely human point of view, the Qur'an considers such a position to be pure delusion, and indeed a great stupidity.

God is the only Creator, and He is absolutely free when He acts. He is, however, serious in His creation:

Did you think We had created you in vain, and that you would
not be brought back to Us? (Q 23:115)

God has created human beings so that they will return to Him, and He has done this with care. As we have seen already, He is *al-khâliq* and *al-muṣawwir*, terms that signify that God has formed humans out of pre-existing matter.

He created mankind out of dried clay, like pottery. (Q 55:14)

Here is another quotation from Abdennour Bidar:

In the Twelfth Century of the Christian era, the theologian Fakhr Din Razi [*sic*] explains that if Allah is called the Creator (*Al-Khâliq*), it is because the Arabic word *khâliq* means both producing, bringing into being (*îjâd*) and determination (*taqdîr*). In other words God is at the same time—and through the very same act—"The One who brings something into existence" and "the One who determines the character of that thing." He is the One who creates something giving it immediately its importance and its place in the universe—for instance in creating a bird, God gives it, at one and the same time, life and its place within nature, as if God were saying to it at the very moment He created it: "You will be the one within my Creation who sings, who flies, and who symbolizes the lightness of the human mind whose ideas rise to the heavens."[4]

We find several times in the Qur'an a meditation on the wonderful creation of the human being. Here is a well-known passage:

We created man from an essence of clay, then We placed him as a drop of fluid in a safe place, then We made that drop into a clinging form, and We made that form into a lump of flesh, and We made that lump into bones, and We clothed those bones with flesh, and later We made him into other forms—glory be to God, the best of creators! *aḥsanu l-khâliqîn*. (Q 23:12-14)

Some clarifications regarding the translation of this text. The "We" refers, of course, to God, for whom the plural of majesty is used. The term for "man" is *al-insân*, which means the human person in general, and not just the male. On the phrase "other forms" Abdel Haleem gives the following note: "(Fakhr al-Din) Razi quotes Ibn Abbas (a companion of Muhammad) to explain 'other forms' as referring to all the various stages of infancy, childhood, and maturity—cf. 22:5; 40:67."[5]

Muslim theologians have discussed at length whether it is possible for there to be other creators besides God, usually to

---

[4] Abdennour Bidar, *L'islam sans soumission. Pour un existentialisme musulman* (Paris: Albin Michel, 2008), pp. 140–41.

[5] The words translated "other forms" are in fact in the singular, *khalq^{an} âkhar*. Yusuf Ali translates "another creature" and adds the following commentary: "From a mere animal, we now consider man as man . . . human life, with all its capacities and responsibilities."

dismiss this possibility. We could say that today, with the progress in biotechnology through which human beings claim to be themselves creators, this verse takes on added meaning.

It is possible also to meditate on the creation of human beings as they are, with all their weaknesses and yet also their wonderful calling:

> How can you ignore God when you were lifeless and He gave you life . . . ? [Prophet], when your Lord told the angels, "I am putting a successor (*khalîfat^(an)*) on earth," they said, "How can You put someone there who will cause damage and bloodshed, when we celebrate your praise and proclaim your holiness?" but He said, "I know things you do not." (Q 2:28, 30)

In the midst of creation the human person is placed as the representative of God, His *khalîfa*.[6] Human beings therefore have duties toward this creation. Yet, God does not leave everything to His representative. He Himself sustains His creation. He is the Provider, *al-razzâq* (Q 51:58). The context in which this Name is found is worth noting:

> I created jinn and mankind only to worship Me: I want no provision (*rizq*) from them, nor do I want them to feed Me. (Q 5:56-57)

God expects from His creatures nothing other than their adoration. It is He who gives the *rizq*, everything that is necessary for

---

[6] On the creation of the human being, see EQ, s.v. "God and His Attributes," pp. 327–28. According to Gerhard Böwering, the author of this article, Adam is the representative on the earth not of God but of the angels, since he has to do what the angels cannot do, which is to name the different creatures (cf. Q 2:31-32).

life on earth.[7] God, however, encourages human beings to look beyond this life, for the Qur'an suggests that there are other good things in store:

> Do not gaze longingly at what We have given some of them to enjoy, the finery of this present life: We test them through this, but the provision (*rizq*) of your Lord is better and more lasting. (Q 20:131)

To sum up, it can be said that God is the Creator, and as Creator He gives special attention to human beings. He sustains life, both in this world and in the world to come.

2. The OT[8]

The Names of God according to the Islamic tradition are often formed from verbs found in the text of the Qur'an. The same procedure could be followed when reading the first account of creation given in Genesis (Gen 1:1–2:4).

- "In the *beginning* when God created" (1:1)—so God can be called the Originator.
- "Then God *said*, 'Let there be light'; and there was light" (1:3). This reminds us of the *kun fa-yakûn* of the Qur'anic text. God has only to say "Be," and the thing exists. This way of creating, through the bare word, is often repeated in this passage from Genesis. The passage continues:
- "And God saw that the light was good; and God *separated* the light from the darkness" (1:4). Further on we find:

[7] Cf. EI2, s.v. "Rizḳ."

[8] On the Names for God as creator in the OT, see ABD, s.v. "Creator."

"And God said, 'Let there be a dome in the midst of the waters, and let it *separate* the waters from the waters'" (1:6). So, in creating, God operates through separation; He is the Separator (*al-fâṭir*).

"God *called* the dome Sky" (1:8)—He gives names to things, thus fixing their nature, and at the same time manifesting His own control over things. Yet He shares this prerogative with the human being He has created (cf. 2:19-20).

"God *set* (the lights) in the dome of the sky" (1:17; see also Ps 8:3: "the moon and the stars that you have *established*").

"God *blessed* (the living creatures)" (1:22)—which means that He gave them life.

At the end of this account special attention is given to the creation of humankind. There is first of all a kind of deliberation:

> God said: "Let us make humankind in our image, according to our likeness." (1:26)

Then God decides that this special creature will have domination over all the others. And finally:

> So God *created* humankind in his image. (1:27)

The special care that God took in creating humankind is underlined in the second account of creation:

> Then the Lord God *formed* man from the dust of the ground,[9] and *breathed* into his nostrils the breath of life, and the man became a living being. (2:7)

---

[9] The *Cambridge Annotated Study Bible* provides a note here giving an alternative translation that brings out the play on words in Hebrew: "formed a man (Heb. *adam*) of dust from the ground (Heb. *adamah*)."

This special interest that God takes in the human being arouses admiration and praise, which are often expressed in the Psalms. Here is just one example, Psalm 8, which begins and ends with the following refrain:

> O Lord, our Sovereign,
> How majestic is your name in all the earth!

The psalmist also exclaims:

> What are human beings that you are mindful of them,
> mortals that you care for them? (Ps 8:1, 4)

The Psalms, in fact, contain numerous references to God as Creator, and through all the verbs of action that are used it is possible to gain an idea of the commitment of God in Creating. Here is an example:

> Bless the Lord, O my soul . . .
> You *stretch out* the heavens like a tent.
> You *set* the beams of your chambers on the waters . . .
> You *set* the earth on its foundations . . .
> You *cover* it with the deep as with a garment. (Ps 104 [103]:1-6)

The same psalm praises God who sustains His creation:

> These all look to you to give them their food in due season;
> When you give it to them, they gather it up;
> When you open your hand, they are filled with good things.
> (Ps 104 [103]:27-28)

In chapter 16 of the book of Exodus we find a portrait of the God who nourishes His people. Responding to the prayer of Moses, God gives the manna. We could note here:

- that each one must gather according to the need felt; there is no absolute uniformity in the amount allowed (it would seem to me that this is often the case when God distributes His gifts);
- that one needs to have confidence in the Lord, so one should not try to accumulate for future needs.

The reflection of a parish priest, quoted by Cardinal Etchegaray, seems apposite here: "In the past, when the people killed a pig, they used always to bring me some pieces of meat. Now that they have the freezer, they keep the lot for themselves."[10]

The OT insists on the fact that God is sole Creator. So the prophet Isaiah declares:

> Thus says the Lord, your Redeemer,
> who formed you in the womb:
> I am the Lord, who made all things,
> who alone stretched out the heavens,
> who by myself spread out the earth. (Isa 44:24; cf. 45:18)

The prophet Jeremiah, for his part, underlines the freedom of God. From the house of the potter he proclaims:

> Can I not do with you, O house of Israel, just as the potter has done? says the Lord. Just like the clay in the potter's hand, so are you in my hand, O house of Israel. (Jer 18:6; cf. Isa 64:7)

This recalls the text of the Qur'an referred to above:

> He created mankind out of dried clay. (Q 55:14)

---

[10] Roger Etchegaray, *J'avance comme un âne: petits clins d'oeil au Ciel et à la terre* (Paris: Fayard, 1984).

Such texts suggest a new Name for God, the Potter.[11] Islamic tradition has not adopted this Name, but it is an image that Paul takes up in his letter to the Romans (cf. Rom 9:20-21).

3. *The NT* [12]

We have thus arrived at the NT, where, as a matter of fact, we find little about creation. This is perhaps because this belief went unchallenged. Paul writes in his letter to the Romans:

> Ever since the creation of the world his eternal power and divine nature, invisible though they are, have been understood and seen through the things he has made. (Rom 1:20)

In his teaching, Jesus puts the accent more on divine providence:

> Consider the lilies of the field, how they grow; they neither toil nor spin, yet I tell you, even Solomon in all his glory was not clothed like one of these. But if God so clothes the grass of the fields, which is alive today and tomorrow is thrown into the oven, will he not much more clothe you—you of little faith? (Matt 6:26-30)

We have seen how God, in his providence, nourished his people by giving them the manna. Following on the passage concerning the manna in Exodus, one could read the discourse of Jesus on the Bread of Life in the Gospel of John, chapter 6. This can be left to the personal initiative of the reader. Here I would like to consider

[11] Peter F. Ellis gives a brief explanation of this Name in his commentary on Jeremiah 18:1-12, in *The Collegeville Bible Commentary* (CBC) (Collegeville, MN: Liturgical Press, 1989), p. 464.

[12] On the Names of God as Creator in the NT, see ABD, s.v. "Creator."

what is said about creation at the beginning of the Gospel of John. According to Christian understanding, creation is attributed to the Word of God, as the prologue to this gospel attests:

> In the beginning was the Word, and the Word was with God, and the Word was God.
> All things came into being through him, and without him not one thing came into being. (John 1:1, 3)

The Word is "at the beginning" not only because of being eternal,[13] existing prior to creation, but also on account of being responsible for the existence of creation. Now since the Word has become flesh, Christian meditation places Jesus at the center of creation, as being at one and the same time its Creator and its final goal. God does not create haphazardly, but according to a definite plan. Here, therefore, by way of conclusion to this meditation, is a text about Jesus from Paul's letter to the Colossians:

> He is the image of the invisible God, the firstborn of all creation; for in him all things in heaven and on earth were created, things visible and invisible . . . all things have been created through him and for him. He himself is before all things, and in him all things hold together. (Col 1:15-20)

It is through Christ and in Christ that creation enjoys coherence.

---

[13] The Word is *azalî*, (pre)-eternal. The Arabic language makes, in fact, a distinction between *azal*, eternity without any beginning, and *abad*, eternity without end. One of the Names of God given in the Shi'ite handbook mentioned in the Introduction is *al-azalî*; cf. *Know Your Islam*, 2nd ed. (Bombay: Anjuman-e-Himayatul Islam, 1970), pp. 24.

What conclusion can be drawn from these texts? We should let ourselves be filled with gratitude, for the gift of life, for our own existence, for the whole of creation that surrounds us and of which we form part. If our sensitivity to the unity of creation grows, then we shall be more inclined to a feeling of confidence and to a desire to give thanks to God in whose hands we are.

II

The Transcendent God

While God is the Manifest or the Patent (*al-ẓâhir*) who makes Himself known through His creation, he is also the Hidden or the Latent (*al-bâṭin*) who cannot be known fully.[1] We are invited to turn our attention to the hidden face of the divinity, recognizing how different God is. Accordingly, the following meditation will be a reflection on divine transcendence and on the holiness of God. This should lead to praise addressed to God for what He is, and not for what He does. It should lead to a form of prayer that is not aimed at obtaining something from God, but is entirely disinterested. Yet, we may discover that God, without our asking, will shower His gifts upon us, for He is the Living One, our true source of Life.

1. *The Teaching of the Qur'an*

We come to know God through His creation. This is the first message of Islam, as we have seen in chapter I. It is also what Paul

---

[1] Cf. EI², s.v. "Al-Ẓahir wa'l-Baṭin," in which it is said that these Names signify that God is both the outward and the inward reality.

teaches in his letter to the Romans. Yet, we find ourselves faced with a paradox: the *invisible* perfection of God is made *manifest*. We know God without really knowing Him. Islam exalts this divine transcendence.

No one is comparable to Him. (Q 112:4)

A number of the Most Beautiful Names express this transcendence:[2]

al-mutakabbir	the Haughty
al-ʿalî	the High
al-kabîr	the Great
al-jalîl	the Majestic
al-mutaʿâlî	the Very High, the Exalted

Muslims often say *subḥân Allâh*: "Glory to God (above everything that one could associate with Him)." This is the reason why, in Islam, theology is called *al-tawḥîd*, declaring the uniqueness of God. It is a defensive theology, because God has to be defended from *shirk*, which means associating something with God, whatever that thing might be. In the eyes of Islam *shirk* is the only sin that really cannot be pardoned.

---

[2] Gimaret examines these Names in the chapter of his book entitled "Parfait" (Gimaret, *Les noms divins*, pp. 201–28). He observes that these attributes bear witness to "the excellence of the Divine Being, His absolute superiority with regard to created beings." He remarks also that divine perfection is expressed essentially through negation: "God is perfect because He is exempt from all imperfection" (p. 201). Al-Ghazâlî discusses these Names in different places in *The Ninety-Nine Beautiful Names*: *al-mutakabbir*, p. 67; *al-ʿalî*, pp. 102–4; *al-kabîr*, pp. 105–6; *al-jalîl*, pp. 112–13; *al-mutaʿâlî*, p. 140.

It is in this context that we should understand the Name "Holy" (*al-quddûs*) attributed to God.[3]

This Name appears only twice in the Qur'an:

> He is God: there is no god other than Him,
> the Controller,[4] the Holy One.   *al-malik al-quddûs*
> (Q 59:23)

> Everything that is in the heavens and earth glorifies God,
> the Controller, the Holy One, the Almighty,
>   the Wise.   *al-malik al-quddûs*
>   (Q 62:1)

Quddûs is the cognate of *qodesh* in Hebrew. Of the latter term it is said: "The Semitic word *qodesh*, a holy thing, holiness, which is derived from a root meaning most probably 'cut' or 'separate,' directs us towards the idea of being set apart from the profane."[5] It could be said that God is "unclassifiable." Consequently, all language applied to God has to be purified. We have, at least, to say that we do not know how the same word (goodness, wisdom, mercy, and so forth) can be applied both to God and to creatures.

---

[3] Cf. Gimaret, *Les noms divins*, pp. 202–4; he refers to Ghazâlî, who says that to qualify God as *quddûs* "is not really to deny any imperfection in Him, since that itself would be tantamount to impugning his dignity, a lack of politeness (*tark al-'adab*); it would be like saying to a king that he is not a carpet-maker or a leach! What it means in fact is that God is beyond all positive qualification, above all perfections that human beings could imagine" (p. 204); cf. al-Ghazâlî, *The Ninety-Nine Beautiful Names*, pp. 59–60.

[4] *Al-malik*: Abdel Haleem suggests in a note the more usual "King/Sovereign"; Yusuf Ali translates "Sovereign." This Name will be reflected on in chapter 5.

[5] Xavier Leon-Dufour, *Vocabulaire de Théologie Biblique*, s.v. "Saint."

As regards the anthropomorphic terms found in the Qur'an, such as "face," "arm," and "hand," Muslim theologians have said that they should be used *bi-lâ kayfa*, "without saying how." This is the negative approach, the apophatic way of the Greek Fathers, which must be respected. We are often too confident in the way we speak about God. A good dose of humility and respect when faced with the immensity of God is very healthy.

As has been noted already, when speaking of the creation of humankind, God is surrounded by a celestial court of angels. The angels proclaim:

> We celebrate Your praise and proclaim
>   Your holiness.   *nuqaddisu la-ka*
>   (Q 2:30)

In other words, they recognize that God is above all created beings.

We are invited to let ourselves be caught up in this movement of praise, for God is also *al-ḥamîd*, "the Praiseworthy." Praise is an essential feature of Islamic spirituality. It is inculcated from the very first *sûra* of the Qur'an, *al-fâtiḥa*:

> Praise belongs to God,
>   Lord of the Worlds   *al-ḥamdu li-Llâhi rabbi l-ᶜâlamîn*
>   (Q 1:2)

It is worth taking note of the distinction between *thanksgiving*, addressed to God on account of His gifts, thanking Him for what He does for us, and *praise*, addressed to God for what He is. The Name *al-ḥamîd* really means that only God truly merits this movement of the soul.

As was observed in the Introduction to these meditations, the Name *al-ḥamîd* is often associated with another Name, *al-ghanî*,[6] the Rich, the Independent, the Self-Sufficient:

Remember that God is
    self-sufficient,
worthy of all praise
    (Q 2:267; cf. 22:64)

    wa-aᶜlamû anna Llâha ghaniyyᵘⁿ
    ḥamîd

People, it is you who stand in need of God—
God needs nothing and is
    worthy of all praise.
    (Q 35:15)

    wa-Llâhu huwa l-ghaniyyu l-ḥamîd

Can one know anything more about this self-sufficient God, about what He is in Himself? The "Verse of the Throne" points the way:

God! There is no God
but He, the Living (*al-ḥayy*);
the Self-Subsisting, Eternal (*al-qayyûm*).[7] (Q 2:255)

---

[6] See p. xxv. The Name *al-ḥamîd* appears seventeen times in the Qur'an, and *al-ghanî* eighteen times, in ten of which they are found together. On these Names see al-Ghazâlî, *The Ninety-Nine Beautiful Names*, p. 143 for *al-ghanî*, pp. 127–28 for *al-ḥamîd*; Gimaret, *Les noms divins*, pp. 222–24.

[7] Translation of Yusuf Ali. It is worth quoting his long note on this verse: "The attributes of God are so different from anything we know in our present world that we have to be content with understanding that the only fit word by which we can name Him is 'He'—the pronoun standing for His name. His name—God or Allâh—is sometimes misused and applied to other beings or things; and we must emphatically repudiate any idea or suggestion that there can be any compeer of

We can say that God is the Living One par excellence, because
He is "the Living [God] who never dies" (Q 25:58), which distinguishes Him from all contingent beings. Moreover, "the Living
One" is the first of the divine attributes, the one that allows Him
to act with power and wisdom.[8]

An invitation is addressed to human beings:

> He is the Living One and there is no god but Him,
> so call on Him, and dedicate your religion
>   entirely to Him.   *mukhalliṣîn la-hu*
>   (Q 40:65)

This means that one should associate nothing with God. No divinity, no other person, no other being is worthy of worship, for
God is the ultimate reason for all things, the final explanation
of existence, the only being that does not owe its existence to
another, the only one that can never disappear.

The Qur'an gives the example of Abraham, who was led by
experience to this pure form of worship:

> In this way We showed Abraham [God's] mighty dominion over
> the heavens and the earth, so that he might be a firm believer.

God. He lives, but His life is self-subsisting and eternal: it does not depend upon
other beings and is not limited to time and space. Perhaps the attribute of *Qaiyûm*
(*sic*) includes not only the idea of 'Self-subsisting' but also the idea of 'Keeping
up and maintaining all life,' His life being the source and constant support of all
derived forms of life." Yusuf Ali, *The Holy Qur'an*, n. 296, p. 102.

[8] Gimaret dedicates a short chapter exclusively to this Name; see *Les noms
divins*, pp. 229–33. He examines the Name *al-qayyûm* in his chapter "Eternel," pp.
188–90. Al-Ghazâlî gives brief commentaries on these Names in *The Ninety-Nine
Beautiful Names*, p. 129 for *al-ḥayy* and pp. 129–30 for *al-qayyûm*.

When the night grew dark over him he saw a star and said, "This is my Lord," but when it set, he said, "I do not like things that set." And when he saw the moon rising he said, "*This* is my Lord," but when it too set, he said, "If my Lord does not guide me, I shall be one of those who go astray." Then he saw the sun rising and cried, "*This* is my Lord! This is greater." *hâdhâ rabbî hâdhâ akbaru* But when the sun set, he said, "My people, I disown all that you worship beside God. I have turned my face as a true believer (*ḥanîf*) towards Him who created the heavens and the earth. I am not one of the polytheists." | *wa-mâ anâ min al-mushrikîn*

(Q 6:75-79)

Can we, like Abraham, become conscious, or renew our consciousness, of the precarious nature of all things and turn our face toward the Eternal One?

This leads us to another Name of God, one that appears only once in the Qur'an, *al-ṣamad*.

Say, "He is God the One,
God the eternal   *al-ṣamad*
(Q 112:1-2)

With regard to the Arabic word *al-ṣamad*, Abdel Haleem adds in a note here that "other commonly held interpretations include 'self-sufficient' and 'sought by all' (Razi)." Yusuf Ali, for his part, has "the Eternal, Absolute." He comments: "*ṣamad* is difficult to translate by one word. I have used two, 'Eternal' and 'Absolute.' The latter implies 1) that absolute existence can only be predicated of Him; all other existence is temporal or conditional; 2) that He is dependent on no person or things, but all persons or things are dependent on Him, thus negativing (*sic*) the idea of gods and goddesses who ate and drank, wrangled and plotted, depended on the gifts of worshippers, etc."[9] Al-Ghazâlî opts for "The Eternal."[10] Louis Gardet, in his article on the Most Beautiful Names of God for the *Encyclopaedia of Islam*, first translates this Name as "the Impenetrable." He then gives a whole gamut of possible renderings: the Master, He who reigns; the one whom the acts of His adversaries neither trouble nor move; the Very High in dignity; the one to whom one prays and addresses supplication; one in whom there is no "hollow," who cannot be divided into parts.[11]

We see, then, that this Name, a *hapax corani*, used only in this passage, is qualifying the One who is Unique. This is confirmed by what follows in the *sûra*:

He begot no one	*lam yalid*
nor was He begotten.	*wa-lam yûlad*
No one is comparable	
to Him.	*wa-lam yakun la-hu kufuw^{an} aḥad*
(Q 112:3-4)	

Is it possible to reconcile all these different interpretations? Is it possible to find one single term that would express all these different shades of meaning? In the qur'anic commentaries on this passage reference is made, by way of example, to a powerful chief who is not the subaltern of any other. One can therefore have recourse to him without fear. He will never be deposed; he will always be there. He is not as the shifting sand, but rather

---

[9] Yusuf Ali, *The Holy Qur'an*, n. 6298, p. 1805.

[10] Cf. Al-Ghazâlî, *The Ninety-Nine Beautiful Names*, p. 131.

[11] EI², s.v. "Al-Asma' Al-Ḥusna." On the difficulty of discerning the true meaning of this Name and the variety of interpretations given by Muslim theologians, see Gimaret, *Les noms divins*, pp. 320–23.

like a solid rock. Here, then, is a possible rendering of *al-ṣamad*: "the Rock." This Name would describe God as being eternal, immutable, indivisible, impassible, and yet One in whom one can always trust, One to whom prayer can always be addressed, One in whom one can ever seek refuge.[12]

2. The OT

In the OT God remains transcendent, even if He intervenes in history and is close to the Chosen People. This transcendence is expressed in the Psalms through the use of the Name "the Most High."[13]

> The Lord also thundered in the heavens,
> and the Most High uttered his voice. (Ps 18 [17]:13)

> Let them know that you alone,
> whose name is the Lord,
> are the Most High over all the earth. (Ps 83 [82]:19)

[12] It was only after I had composed this meditation that I discovered that Michel Cuypers had arrived at the same conclusion. Moreover, he found confirmation of the choice of "the Rock" to translate *al-ṣamad* in a modern commentary on the Qur'an in Urdu; cf. Michel Cuypers, "Une lecture rhétorique et intertextuelle de la Sourate al-Ikhlâṣ," in MIDEO, 25–26 (2004), pp. 142–43, and see the whole article with the relevant bibliography, pp. 141–75. Michael Sells has also proposed "the Rock" along with "forever" and "the refuge" in his three versions of *sûrat al-ikhlâṣ*; he notes, moreover, the existence of the word *ṣamada*, meaning a large rock; cf. Michael Sells, *Approaching the Qur'an*, 2nd ed. (Ashland, OR: White Cloud Press, 2007), pp. 136–37.

[13] *Elyôn*. This Name, which had fallen into disuse, was revived during the period following the Exile in order to emphasize the divine transcendence; cf. ABD, s.v. "Most High."

This leads the psalmist to exclaim:

> I will give to the Lord the thanks due to his righteousness,
> and sing praise to the name of the Lord, the Most High. (Ps 7:17)

It would be possible to continue with similar quotations, but it seems preferable to concentrate on the three Names that have come up in the qur'anic section of this chapter.

The Living God

According to the biblical account, Moses died before the people of Israel entered the Promised Land. It fell to Joshua, the commander that Moses had appointed, to lead the people into the land. Joshua had the Ark of the Covenant carried in the van of the procession as a sign of God's promise that He would accompany His people. Joshua said:

> By this you will know that among you is the living God.
> (Josh 3:10)

In the book of Jeremiah we find this Name used together with others:

> But the Lord is the true God;
> He is the living God, and the everlasting King. (Jer 10:10)

It is worthwhile paying attention to the context in which this strong affirmation is to be found. The prophet has just spoken about the worship of idols, a practice that he rejects completely. The idols are false gods; they have nothing of the truth, in contrast to the True God. These idols, he says, are like "scarecrows" (v. 5); they are both "stupid" and "foolish" (v. 8) (this would correspond to the qur'anic term *bâṭil*). Jeremiah severely reprimands those who are not faithful to God. In another place he cries out to the Lord:

> O hope of Israel! O Lord!
> All who forsake you shall be put to shame;
> those who turn away from you shall be recorded in the underworld,
> for they have forsaken the fountain of living water, the Lord.
>   (Jer 17:13)

Earlier on he had announced to the people the word of the Lord:

> For my people have committed two evils:
> they have forsaken me,
> the fountain of living water,
> and dug out cisterns for themselves,
> cracked cisterns
> that can hold no water. (Jer 2:13)

Source of true life, God is indeed worthy of this Name, the Living God. This is the Name that King Darius uses for the God of Daniel:

> May you have abundant prosperity. I make a decree, that in all my royal dominion people should tremble and fear before the God of Daniel:
>
> For he is the living God,
> enduring forever.
> His kingdom shall never be destroyed,
> and his dominion has no end. (Dan 6:25-26)

The Holy One

The proclamation of the All Holy God[14] is found in an outstanding way in the vision granted to the prophet Isaiah:

> I saw the Lord sitting on a throne, high and lofty; and the hem
> of his robe filled the temple. Seraphs were in attendance above
> him. . . .
> And one called to another and said:
> "Holy, holy, holy is the Lord of hosts;
> The whole earth is full of his glory." (Isa 6:1-3)

To this passage could be compared the "Verse of the Throne" in *sûrat al-baqara* (Q 2:254).

The prophet Isaiah often speaks of the "Holy One of Israel" (cf. Isa 1:4; 5:19; 5:24; and *passim*). In a prophecy that is probably concerned with the invasion of Sennacherib, he describes vividly the way the Lord acts:

> The light of Israel will become a fire,
> and his Holy One a flame;
> and it will burn and devour
> his thorns and briars in one day. (Isa 10:17)

It is obvious from this how demanding is the holiness of God, since it destroys everything that is opposed to it.

This way of naming God, as the Holy One of Israel, may appear to be too exclusive. In the other sections of the book of Isaiah, however, in the Book of the Consolation of Israel (or Second

---

[14] God is considered to be the ideal manifestation of holiness, and indeed its source; the people are enjoined to emulate God by keeping the commandments; cf. ABD, s.v. "Holiness."

Isaiah, chaps. 40–55) and in Third Isaiah (chaps. 56–66), a degree
of religious universalism appears.[15]

> The Holy One of Israel is your Redeemer,
> the God of the whole earth he is called. (Isa 54:5)

It is probably the experience of the covenant between God and His
people that affords us the best understanding of the holiness of God.
In chapter 19 of Exodus it is related how God, wishing to sanctify
His people, gave them, through Moses, detailed instructions. They
are to purify themselves. In actual fact, the people are afraid of
God, and it is Moses who approaches Him in their name while
they remain apart. In chapter 24, at the time of the ratification of
the covenant, Moses is able to enter the cloud, which represents the
glory of God, without suffering any harm. Chapter 33 shows the
intimate relationship between God and His servant Moses, who can
speak to Him face to face (in the Islamic tradition Moses is known
as *kalîm Allâh,* the one with whom God used to speak directly).
God calls Moses by his name, and Moses wishes to know the Name
of God. In the following chapter God reveals Himself to Moses:

> The Lord, the Lord,
> a God merciful and gracious,
> slow to anger,
> and abounding in steadfast love and faithfulness. (Exod 34:6)

At the same time, while promising to do marvels for the people,
God reveals how demanding the relationship with Him is:

---

[15] Cf. the introduction to Isaiah in *The Jerusalem Bible* (London: Darton,
Longman & Todd, 1966), p. 1125.

> You shall worship no other god, because the Lord, whose name is Jealous, is a jealous God. (Exod 34:14)

God will brook no rival.

The book of Leviticus insists on the requirements of holiness. After a whole series of prescriptions concerning food, which can be clean or unclean, we find the following text:

> You shall not make yourselves detestable with any creature that swarms; you shall not defile yourselves with them, and so become unclean. For I am the Lord your God; sanctify yourselves therefore, and be holy, for I am holy. You shall not defile yourselves with any swarming creature that moves on the earth. For I am the Lord who brought you out from the land of Egypt, to be your God; you shall be holy, for I am holy. (Lev 11:43-45)

And again we find the same command:

> The Lord spoke to Moses, saying: Speak to all the congregation of the people of Israel and say to them: You shall be holy, for I the Lord your God am holy. (Lev 19:1-2)

The *Traduction Oecuménique de la Bible* provides a note on this passage: "The common denominator in all these different precepts is the holiness of God, which is to become manifest in all the acts and in all the circumstances of the life of the people who are *consecrated* (*qadosh*), that is made holy, to the God who is Holy (*qadosh*)."[16]

---

[16] *Traduction Oecuménique de la Bible, Ancien Testament* (Paris: Cerf, 1975), p. 236, n. *l*.

The Rock

That God can bear no rival forms an essential part of the message of the Qur'an, forcefully expressed in *sûrat al-ikhlâṣ*, which mentions the Name *al-ṣamad,* translated above as the Rock.[17]

This Name, the Rock, is very familiar to Christians. It is found in the psalm used in the Office as the invitatory for the first prayer of the day:

> O come, let us sing to the Lord;
> let us make a joyful noise to the rock of our salvation!
> (Ps 95 [94]:1)[18]

Elsewhere it is found linked with other Names:

> I love you, O Lord, my strength.
> The Lord is my rock, my fortress, and my deliverer,
> my God, my rock in whom I take refuge,
> my shield, and the horn of my salvation, my stronghold.
>   (Ps 18 [17]:1-2)

This theme of God as the Rock is developed in a very rich way in the Song of Moses, which is found in chapter 32 of Deuteronomy:

---

[17] Mircea Eliade has drawn attention to the fascination of the rock: by the very fact that it *exists*, that it *endures*, that it is *fixed in immobility*, it suggests to human beings the idea of something that overcomes and transcends the precariousness of human existence, and even an absolute manner of being. It is easy, therefore, to understand how the notion of sacredness can become attached to a rock, not for the sake of the rock itself, but on account of its relationship with Another; cf. the chapter on sacred stones in *Patterns in Comparative Religion* (London: Sheed and Ward, 1958).

[18] Unfortunately the Grail version of the Psalms used in the *Divine Office* translates: "Come, ring out our joy to the Lord; hail the God who saves us."

> The Rock, his work is perfect,
> and all his ways are just.
> A faithful God, without deceit,
> just and upright is he. (Deut 32:4)

This description evokes some of the Beautiful Names of God: *al-muqsiṭ*, the Equitable; *al-mu'min*, the Believer, or rather the Faithful One, the source of security and protection; *al-ʿadl*, the Just.

The Song of Moses continues with a strong criticism of the people of Israel:

> Jeshurun grew fat, and kicked[19] . . .
> He abandoned God who made him,
> and scoffed at the Rock of his salvation . . .
> You were unmindful of the Rock that bore you;[20]
> you forgot the God who gave you birth. (Deut 32:15-18)

The contrast with *sûrat al-ikhlâṣ* is striking. While the qur'anic text, insisting on the transcendence of God, eliminates all possibility of begetting, the Rock that is God in the Bible is strangely able to beget.

3. *The NT*

The same three Names that have been dealt with above will be considered here also.

---

[19] The JB explains in a note: "Like a bull, *shor*; the word *Jeshurun*, applied to Israel here and in 33:5, alludes to this, but is of uncertain derivation," p. 259, n. *g*.

[20] The *Cambridge Annotated Study Bible* gives in a note an alternative translation, "that begot you," which is probably closer to the original.

The Living God

It would seem that in the time of Jesus it was fairly common to refer to God as "the living God." In the presence of the whole Sanhedrin, the High Priest presses Jesus to state clearly who he is:

> I put you under oath before the living God, tell us if you are the Messiah, the Son of God. (Matt 26:63)

In reply, Jesus proclaims his identity:

> Jesus said to him: "You have said so. But I tell you,
> From now on you will see the Son of Man
> seated at the right hand of Power
> and coming on the clouds of heaven." (Matt 26:64)

Previously, in answering a question about the resurrection put to him by the Sadducees, Jesus had spoken to them about God who is not a God of the dead, but of the living (cf. Matt 22:32).

We find the term *the living God* in the writings of Saint Paul also. Speaking about conversion, he writes to the Thessalonians:

> For the people of those regions report about us what kind of welcome we had among you, and how you turned to God from idols, to serve a living and true God, and to wait for his Son from heaven, whom he raised from the dead—Jesus, who rescues us from the wrath that is coming. (1 Thess 1:9-10)

I would like to call attention to the verb that Paul uses here: "turned." If the new converts to Christianity had turned to God, it was because God Himself had first turned to humanity through his Son, Jesus Christ. Among the Beautiful Names of God is to be found *al-tawwâb*, the Repentant, or the One who is habitually turning toward His creatures.

God manifests Himself through His Word.

> In the beginning was the Word,
> and the Word was turned toward God,
> and what God was the Word also was . . .
> In him was life
> and the life was the light of humankind. (John 1:1-4)[21]

Jesus, the Word made flesh, proclaims himself to be Life.

> I am the resurrection and the life. Those who believe in me, even
> though they die, will live. (John 11:25)

> I am the way, the truth, and the life. (John 14:6)

It is only natural, then, for Peter to proclaim, in the name of all the disciples, his faith in Jesus in these terms:

> You are the Messiah, the Son of the living God. (Matt 16:16)

Or again:

> Lord, to whom can we go? You have the words of eternal life.
> (John 6:68)

Peter, when preaching to the crowd that had gathered after the cure of a crippled beggar in the Temple, speaks of Jesus as "the

---

[21] The translation here is that provided by Francis J. Moloney in *The Gospel of John*, Sacra Pagina (Collegeville, MN: Liturgical Press, 1998), p. 33. Moloney explains: "The Word preexists the human story, and the Word does not preexist for its own sake but in a relationship with God (*pros ton theon*). The preposition *pros* means more than the static 'with.' It has a sense of motion toward the person or thing that follows. The translation therefore reads 'the Word was *turned toward* God.' There is a dynamism in the relationship that must somehow be conveyed" (p. 35).

Author of Life." Jesus is the one who, by his Cross and Resurrection, has led his disciples to faith, salvation and life.[22]

The Holy One

This Name does not appear very frequently in the NT. It is present, however, in what could be called an equivalent fashion.[23] For example, Jesus addresses God as "Holy Father" (John 17:11). In the prayer that he taught his disciples he makes a link between the Name of God and holiness:

> Our Father in heaven,
> hallowed be your name. (Matt 6:9)

Mary, in the *Magnificat*, declares:

> For the Mighty One has done great things for me,
> And holy is his name. (Luke 1:49)

At the time of the Annunciation, Mary had heard the angel explaining to her how it would be possible for her to conceive a child while remaining a virgin:

> The Holy Spirit will come upon you, and the power of the Most High will overshadow you; therefore the child to be born will be holy; he will be called Son of God. (Luke 1:35)

We see, then, that the three Persons of the Blessed Trinity are all called holy: Holy Father, the Holy Spirit, and Jesus, the Son of God, is also called holy.

---

[22] Cf. ABD, s.v. "Author of Life."
[23] Cf. ABD, s.v. "Holiness (NT)."

As we have seen in the Gospel of John, in what is known as his "priestly" prayer, Jesus addresses God as "Holy Father" (John 17:11). Moloney comments: Jesus "asks God to care for his fragile disciples, to be 'father' to them. Finally, in v. 17, picking up the theme of the holiness of God, Jesus asks that he sanctify the disciples, making them holy as Jesus is holy."[24] The *Traduction Oecuménique de la Bible* notes that the invocation "Holy Father" was used very early on in Christian liturgy (*Didaché* 10:2).[25]

We find that the holiness of Jesus is recognized by the demons. An unclean spirit cries out:

> What have you to do with us, Jesus of Nazareth? Have you come to destroy us? I know who you are, the Holy One of God. (Mark 1:24)

The declaration of Peter after the discourse of Jesus on the Bread of Life has already been mentioned. After having recognized that with Jesus are the words of life, Peter continues:

> We have come to believe and know that you are the Holy One of God. (John 6:69).

In a prayer that the first Christians addressed to the Father, we find Jesus called "your holy servant" (Acts 4:27). Beforehand, Peter, in one of his first discourses, accused the crowd, saying:

> But you rejected the Holy and Righteous One and asked to have a murderer given to you, and you killed the Author of life, whom God raised from the dead. To this we are witnesses. (Acts 3:14-15)

[24] *Gospel of John*, p. 465.
[25] Cf. *Traduction Oecuménique de la Bible (NT)*, p. 342, n. *k*.

The First Letter of Peter, recalling the demands made by the first covenant between God and the chosen people, gives a reminder that holiness is a required consequence of conversion to Christ:

> Like obedient children, do not be conformed to the desires that you formerly had in ignorance. Instead, as he who called you is holy, be holy yourselves in all your conduct; for it is written, "You shall be holy, for I am holy." (1 Pet 1:14-16)

Finally, in the book of Revelation, a vision is presented of the heavenly liturgy that is celebrated around the throne of God. It echoes the vision of the prophet Isaiah:

> Holy, holy, holy,
> The Lord God the Almighty,
> Who was and is and is to come. (Rev 4:8)

When the Lamb opens the fifth seal of the book with seven seals, the Christian martyrs who are in the sacred precinct, close to God, cry out in a loud voice:

> Sovereign Lord, holy and true, how long will it be before you judge and avenge our blood upon the inhabitants of the earth? (Rev 6:10)

It is to Jesus, however, that judgment is entrusted, for, risen from the dead, Jesus is seated at the right hand of the Father, and it is there that he, the Holy One, will hold judgment:

> These are the words of the holy one, the true one,
> who has the key of David,
> who opens and no one will shut,
> who shuts and no one will open. (Rev 3:7)

The Rock

The theme of the Rock is scarcely present in the NT. We have to arrive at it in a rather roundabout way.

Jesus, in the Temple, declares:

> "Let anyone who is thirsty come to me. And let the one who believes in me drink. As the scripture has said, 'Out of the believer's heart shall flow rivers of living water.'" Now he said this about the Spirit, which believers in him were to receive. (John 7:37-39)

These words were an echo of a rite that was accomplished during the Feast of Tabernacles, a prayer for rain. It recalled an episode in the OT in which the people demanded water and Moses had to strike the rock, from which water flowed out. According to a midrash, the rock accompanied the people on their journey across the Sinai desert. Paul takes up this theme in his letter to the Corinthians:

> All ate the same spiritual food, and all drank the same spiritual drink. For they drank from the spiritual rock that followed them, and the rock was Christ. (1 Cor 10:3-4)

In other words, Paul is reminding Christians that they are to find their nourishment in Christ, and find in him the water of life.

There is also the theme of the "cornerstone" or "keystone" as a figure for Christ. After having told the parable of the wicked tenants who put to death the heir of the owner in order to seize the inheritance (cf. Matt 21:33-39), Jesus explains the parable, indirectly identifying himself with the heir by quoting Psalm 118:

> The stone that the builders rejected
> has become the chief cornerstone.

This is the LORD's doing;
it is marvelous in our eyes. (Ps 118 [117]:22-23)

Peter takes up this quotation in his speech before the Sanhedrin, adding, referring to Jesus whom the rulers of the people had put to death:

> There is salvation in no one else, for there is no other name under heaven given among mortals by which we must be saved. (Acts 4:12)

The image of the cornerstone appears also in the First Letter of Peter:

> Come to him, a living stone, though rejected by mortals yet chosen and precious in God's sight, and like living stones, let yourselves be built into a spiritual house, to be a holy priesthood, to offer spiritual sacrifices acceptable to God through Jesus Christ. (1 Pet 2:4-5)

The text continues, quoting the passage from Psalm 118 and also a passage from Isaiah (Isa 28:16). Christ is identified as the cornerstone, the foundation stone that makes the building strong. At the same time he is a living stone, for the risen Christ is the source of life who allows all those who are incorporated into him to be themselves living stones.

We may draw the conclusion that the Names used for God in the OT, the living God, the Holy One, the Rock, are now applied to Jesus. He is the foundation of Christian life. The command given of old, "Be holy as your heavenly Father is holy," will be fulfilled in conforming one's life to that of Jesus.

III
God with Us

God, the Creator of heaven and earth, of all things visible and invisible, God, the Almighty, even if He is the Most High, the Holy One, the transcendent God, does not remain remote from His creation. He is close to us; He sees everything; He knows us intimately. It is good to strengthen this awareness of the proximity of the One who is truly Emmanuel, God-with-us.

1. *The Teaching of the Qur'an*

In the text of the Qur'an that lists a number of the Beautiful Names of God (cf. Q 59:22-23), there are two that are difficult to translate, *al-mu'min* and *al-muhaymin*.[1]

---

[1] Cf. al-Ghazâlî, *The Ninety-Nine Beautiful Names*, pp. 62–63, for *al-mu'min*, and p. 64 for *al-muhaymin*. Gimaret discusses these Names in his chapter entitled "Sûr," that is, "Certain." He introduces the chapter in the following way: "Certain, that is to say that God is worthy of trust. God is true. He keeps His promises; all can put their trust in Him with complete security," (*Les noms divins*, p. 357). The explanation of *al-mu'min* is found on pp. 359–61, while that of *al-muhaymin* is on pp. 361–63.

Al-mu'min would normally translate as "the Believer," but this hardly seems appropriate for God. Louis Gardet notes that some Muslim theologians have seen in this Name an indication of God's uncreated faith in Himself. He is the One who "authenticates Himself and authenticates His Messenger by His supreme Veracity." Gardet notes, however, an alternative interpretation: "The One who gives security," *amân*.[2] Yusuf Ali prefaces his explanation of this passage from the Qur'an with the following words: "How can a translator reproduce the sublimity and the comprehensiveness of the magnificent Arabic words, which mean so much in a single symbol?" He then explains *al-mu'min*: "one who entertains Faith, who gives Faith to others, who is never false to the Faith that others place in him: hence our paraphrase 'Guardian of the Faith.'"[3] Abdel Haleem proposes "Granter of Security," without further comment.

The last-mentioned translation receives confirmation from the connection of this Name to *al-muhaymin*, translated by Abdel Haleem as "Guardian over all" and by Yusuf Ali as "the Preserver of Safety." We find this term in Q 5:48 in the context of the sending down of the Qur'an, which is said to confirm the Scriptures that came before it, preserving them from all alteration. God watches over both His creation and His revelation.

The nearness of God to His creatures is often expressed in the Qur'an. There is, for instance, the well-known text:

> We created man—We know what his soul whispers to him: We are closer to him than his jugular vein. (Q 50:16)

[2] Cf. EI², s.v. " al-Asma' al-Husna."
[3] Yusuf Ali, *The Holy Qur'an*, n. 5402, p. 1528.

Even if the text appears within the context of judgment, it shows how near God is to His creature.

There are other texts that emphasize the close attention that God pays to human beings:

> [Prophet], if my servants ask you about Me, I am near. I respond to those who call Me, so let them respond to Me, and believe in Me, so that they may be guided. (Q 2:186)

The Arabic prophet Sâlih proclaims the One God to his people, saying:

> My people, worship God. You have no God other than Him. It was He who brought you into being from the earth and made you inhabit it, so ask forgiveness from Him, and turn back to Him: my Lord is near, and ready to answer.   *inna rabbî qarîb^{un} mujîb*
> (Q 11:61)

Similarly Muhammad is given this command:

> Say, "If I go astray, that is my loss, and if I am rightly guided, it is through what my Lord has revealed to me. He is all hearing, and ever near.   *inna-hu samî^{cun} qarîb*
> (Q 34:50)

Qarîb is not found in the list of the Names used as a basis for these meditations, but it does figure in other lists. There are also other Names that give expression to divine proximity:

Al-ʿalîm	the All-Knowing;
Al-baṣîr	the All-Seeing;
Al-samîʿ	the All-Hearing;

Al-khabîr	the Sagacious, or the Well-Informed;
Al-mujîb	the One who answers prayers.[4]

In a context dealing with the way married people should behave, it is said:

God is watchful over all (Q 33:52)	*wa-kâna Llâhu ʿalâ kulli shayʾin raqîbᵃⁿ*

This is not difficult for God, for He is the One who is present (*al-shahîd*), the Witness.[5]

The People of the Book, who do not wish to believe in the signs given by God, are reminded:

God witnesses everything you do (Q 3:98)	*wa-Llâhu shahîdᵘⁿ ʿalâ mâ taʿmalûna*

This knowledge that God has as a Witness will be important, especially on the Day of Judgment:

> We have revealed clear messages, and humiliating torment awaits those who ignore them, on the Day when God will raise everyone and make them aware of what they have done. God has taken account of it all, though they may have forgotten: He witnesses everything (*wa-Llâhu ʿalâ kulli shayʾin shahîd*).

---

[4] Cf. al-Ghazâlî, *The Ninety-Nine Beautiful Names*, pp. 80–81 for *al-ʿalîm*, pp. 84–85 for *al-baṣîr*, pp. 83–84 for *al-samîʿ*, pp. 98–99 for *al-khabîr*, and pp. 115–16 for *al-mujîb*. Gimaret examines these Names in the chapter titled "Omniscient," the All-Knowing, *Les noms divins*, pp. 253–78, except for *al-mujîb*, which is classified among the Names expressing God's generosity, pp. 406–7.

[5] Cf. al-Ghazâlî, *The Ninety-Nine Beautiful Names*, p. 123; Gimaret, *Les noms divins*, pp. 268–69.

> Do you not see [Prophet] that God knows everything in the heavens and earth? There is no secret conversation between three people where He is not the fourth, nor between five where He is not the sixth, nor between less or more than that without Him being with them, wherever they may be. On the Day of Resurrection, He will show them what they have done: God has full knowledge of everything. (Q 58:5-7)

As is well known, witnessing (*shahâda*) is a constituent component of Islam: it is through pronouncing the *shahâda*, the formula of faith, that one becomes a Muslim. In the Qur'an, however, we find that it is God who is the first to bear witness:

> God bears witness (*shahida Llâhu*) that there is no god but Him, as do the angels and those who have knowledge. He upholds justice. There is no god but Him, the Almighty the All Wise. (Q 3:18)

God said to Moses:

> I have chosen you, so listen to what is being revealed. I am God; there is no god but Me, so worship Me and keep up the prayer so that you remember Me. (Q 20:14)

We could say that God is the only one who has the necessary purity and holiness to be able to proclaim worthily his own Oneness. Yet God associates human beings in this witness of faith.

> [Prophet], when your Lord took out the offspring from the loins of the Children of Adam and made them bear witness about themselves, He said, "Am I not your Lord?" and they replied "Yes, we bear witness."   *qâlû balâ shahidnâ*
> (Q 7:172)

This is a text dealing with the pre-eternal pact (*mîthâq*) established with the whole of humanity. Its teaching is that natural religion (*fiṭra*) is monotheism, *islâm* in the sense of submission to the One God.[6] The role of the prophets will be simply to recall this primal pact, this natural faith, for human beings are naturally inclined to forgetfulness (following the Arabic saying *al-insân nâs^in* —the human being is forgetful).

In the course of their mission the prophets meet with opposition. Noah was mocked; the preaching of Hud was not listened to; the camel of Salih was hamstrung; Shuʿayb was threatened with stoning (cf. Q 11:23sq.) But God was with His prophets:

He said: "Then bear witness, and I too will bear witness." (Q 3:81)	*qâla fa-shhadû wa-anâ maʿa-kum mina l-shâhidîn*

A more literal translation of the second part of this phrase would be "and I am with you among those who bear witness." This "being with" of God gives a community dimension to witness.

> God has called you Muslims (*al-muslimîna*)—both in the past and in this [message]—so that the Messenger can bear witness about you (*li-yakûna l-rasûlu shahîd^an ʿalay-kum*) and so that you can bear witness about other people (*wa-takûnû shuhadâʾa ʿalâ l-nâs*).

The preposition used after the term *witness*, in the case both of the Prophet and of the Muslims, is *ʿalâ*, which can mean "on" or "against." Of course in the greeting *al-salâmu ʿalay-kum*, the meaning is positive, "Peace be upon you." Despite the possible negative meaning in the qur'anic text—to witness against—what is recalled here is a duty in some way similar to the duty incumbent on the Muslim community of ordering what is good and

[6] Cf. EI², s.v. "Mithak."

forbidding what is reprehensible (*al-ʿamr bi-l-maʿrûf wa-l-nahy ʿani l-munkar*).

> [Believers], you are the best community singled out for people: you order what is right, forbid what is wrong, and believe in God. (Q 3:110)

This can be connected with a well-known verse:

> We have made you [believers] into a just community, so that you may bear witness [to the truth] before others and so that the Messenger may bear witness [to it] before you. (Q 2:143)[7]

The Islamic community receives a vocation, a mission, which is to be accomplished with the help of God and which, in fact, implies no superiority.

2. The OT

God with Us

Here is an episode from the life of Isaac that is recounted in Genesis. There is famine in the land, but God shows Isaac what he is to do:

> Do not go down to Egypt; settle in the land that I shall show you. Reside in this land as an alien, and I will be with you, and will bless you. (Gen 26:2-3)

---

[7] The expression "just community" translates the Arabic *ummat^{an} wasat^{an}*. This means literally, as Abdel Haleem points out in a note, "'a middle nation,' which some take to mean moderate.'" It may be noticed that the translator has introduced the idea of the truth to which witness is to be given, an idea that could be said to be under the surface of the Arabic text.

In fact, with the help of the Lord's blessing, Isaac does indeed become rich (Gen 26:13). After several disputes concerning access to water have occurred, God renews His covenant:

> [Isaac] went up to Beer-sheba. And that very night the Lord appeared to him and said: "I am the God of your father Abraham; do not be afraid, for I am with you and will bless you and make your offspring numerous for my servant Abraham's sake." So he built an altar there, called on the name of the Lord, and pitched his tent there. (Gen 26:23-25)

Isaac is conscious of the presence of the Lord, but he feels the need to mark the spot by leaving a memorial. It will be possible for him to return there to remind himself that the Lord is with him. We also need such markers, whether they be to places of pilgrimage, or to places where we have had some special religious experience. They may also be reminders of moments in our life when we have had an experience of the Lord, moments to which we can return, at least in spirit.

Jacob's dream (Gen 28:10-22) is another example of the presence of God. He dreams that the Lord is standing beside him, saying:

> Know that I am with you and will keep you wherever you go, and will bring you back to this land; for I will not leave you until I have done what I have promised you. (Gen 28:15)

Then Jacob, rising in the morning, set up a stone as a pillar, and called the place *Beth-El*, the House of God, where worship could be given to God.

Let us return to the episode of the burning bush that we considered in the introductory meditation. Moses receives a mission to go to Pharaoh so that his people may be freed. He is alarmed by this. But God says to him: "I am with you." When Moses asks God to reveal His Name, God replies: "I am who I am" or, according to a different translation, "I will be what I will be" (Exod 3:12-14). This laconic and enigmatic way of replying can be understood in different ways: "I am who I am"—I do not want to tell you who I am; "I am what I am" or "I am the One who is"—in contrast to the false gods who are nothing; "I am who I shall be"—I am there with you in a way that will become evident.[8]

The call of Gideon furnishes another example (cf. Judg 6:11-24). The angel of the Lord calls to Gideon and addresses him: "The Lord is with you, mighty warrior." Gideon protests: he has not experienced the presence of the Lord. The Lord, however, entrusts him with a mission, but he feels incapable of carrying it out. The Lord therefore comforts him: "But I will be with you." Gideon verifies the divine promise by putting the Lord to the test. Finally he is convinced, and he regains his peace of mind. The Lord says to him: "Peace be to you; do not fear, you shall not die." "Then Gideon built an altar there to the Lord, and called it, The Lord is peace." (Judg 6:24).

We may also recall the First Song of the Servant, in Isaiah, where the Lord says:

---

[8] See the different renderings possible in *The Cambridge Annotated Study Bible*, p. 48, nn. *e* and *f*. On this Name of God see ABD, s.v. "Yahweh (Deity)," where it is said that the meaning of the Name YHWH is not clear. It may be derived from *hâwây*, a more ancient form of *hâyâh*, "to be," understood theologically as signifying "the One who is" or "the One who exists" or "the One who causes existence."

But you, Israel, my servant,
>   Jacob whom I have chosen,
>   the offspring of Abraham, my friend;
> you whom I took from the ends of the earth,
>   and called from the farthest corners,
> saying to you: "You are my servant,
>   I have chosen you and not cast you off";
> do not fear, for I am with you,
>   do not be afraid, for I am your God;
> I will strengthen you, I will help you.
> I will uphold you with my victorious right hand. (Isa 41:8-10)

A little further on in the same chapter we find this profession that God makes of his own identity, which is at the same time a promise:

> For I, the LORD your God,
> hold your right hand;
> it is I who say to you, "Do not fear,
> I will help you." (Isa 41:13)

The Lord's presence is a guarantee of his help.

3. *The NT*

God with Us

The promise that God will be with us is constant in the NT. It is found in the angel's message to Mary at the Annunciation: "Greetings, favored one, the Lord is with you," and then: "The Holy Spirit will come upon you, and the power of the Most High will overshadow you" (cf. Luke 1:26-38).

It is found also in the message given to Joseph (cf. Matt 1:18-24). "Joseph, son of David, do not be afraid to take Mary as your wife, for the child conceived in her is from the Holy Spirit." Joseph is instructed to give to this son who will be born of Mary the name Jesus. But the child receives another name also, in fulfillment of the prophecy: "Look, the virgin shall conceive and bear a son, and they shall call him Emmanuel" (quoting Isa 7:14). The evangelist explains this Name: "God is with us."[9] Jesus will remain Emmanuel, even after his death and resurrection. When sending his disciples to bring the good news to the entire world, he promises them: "And remember, I am with you always, to the end of the age" (Matt 28:20).

Yet Jesus is not only *with* us; he is also *in* us. Speaking to his disciples after the Last Supper, he assures them:

> I will not leave you orphaned; I am coming to you. In a little while the world will no longer see me, but you will see me; because I live, you also will live. On that day you will know that I am in my Father, and you in me, and I in you. (John 14:18-20)

The Gospel of John continues with the image of the vine (John 15:1-17), where the verb *abide* is used eleven times. "Abide in me as I abide in you" (v. 4). We have there, in an outstanding way, an expression of the communion to which the meditation on the Names of God can lead us.

God, the Witness

Let us return for a moment to the Qur'an. In *sûrat al-mâ'ida,* "The Feast," we find the following passage, which gives its name to the *sûra*:

> When the disciples said, "Jesus, son of Mary, can your Lord send down a feast to us from heaven?" he said, "Beware of God if you are true believers." They said, "We wish to eat from it; to have our

---

[9] On this Name see ABD, s.v. "Immanuel. "

hearts reassured; to know that you have told us the truth; and to
be witnesses of it."   *wa-nakûna ʿalay-hâ min al-shâhidîn*
(Q 5:112-13)

It should be noted that what is requested is food for the heart
rather than for the body. It is to be a sign—we would be tempted
to say a sacrament—of the truth of which the disciples are to be
witnesses. Perhaps for them, as for us, it is not sufficient to be
present and to share in this meal; there is also a call to bear witness to it, declaring its true meaning: "We proclaim your death,
Lord Jesus, until you come again."

Can we say that God Himself is a witness, the first witness? In
the First Letter of John God is seen to manifest His own nature:

> Whoever does not love does not know God, for God is love. God's
> love was revealed among us in this way: God sent his only Son
> into the world so that we might live through him. (1 John 4:8-9)

The Father bears witness to the Son through the works that the
Son is given to perform (cf. John 5:36 and the whole passage).
He gives witness to him, in word, at the moment of the baptism
of Jesus, saying:

> You are my Son, the Beloved; with you I am well pleased.
> (Luke 3:22)

And again at the transfiguration:

> This is my Son, my Chosen; listen to him. (Luke 9:35)

This witness of the Father becomes definitive after the Resurrection of the Son,

> who was descended from David according to the flesh and was
> declared to be Son of God with power according to the spirit of
> holiness by resurrection from the dead, Jesus Christ our Lord.
> (Rom 1:3-4)

Jesus himself is a witness. He gave witness to the truth before Pontius Pilate (cf. 1 Tim 6:13; John 18:33-38). It could be said that he bore witness through the gift of himself on the Cross, when he emptied himself, humbled himself, becoming obedient even to the point of death (cf. Phil 2:6-11). He is "the faithful witness" (Rev 1:5).

We, for our part, are called to share in this witness:

> But you will receive power when the Holy Spirit has come upon you; and you will be my witnesses in Jerusalem, in all Judea and Samaria, and to the ends of the earth. (Acts 1:8)

This witness includes an appeal to a life of communion, joyful sharing, in a trinitarian climate:

> This life was revealed, and we have seen it and testify to it, and declare to you the eternal life that was with the Father and was revealed to us—we declare to you what we have seen and heard so that you also may have fellowship with us; and truly our fellowship is with the Father and with his Son Jesus Christ. (1 John 1:2-3)

The Holy Spirit is not mentioned explicitly here, but is present implicitly, for there can be no true communion without the Spirit.

And if the witness is not made welcome? Then patience and discretion will be required.

> Always be ready to make your defense to anyone who demands from you an accounting for the hope that is in you; yet do it with gentleness and reverence. (1 Pet 3:15)

> Conduct yourselves honorably among the Gentiles, so that, though they may malign you as evildoers, they may see your honorable deeds and glorify God when he comes to judge. (1 Pet 2:12)

It could be said that it is life itself, a life lived in obedience to God, that is to bear witness.

IV

The God of Goodness and Mercy

The Creator God, the God Most High, is also the God-with-us. He is All-Knowing; He knows of what we are made; He knows our weaknesses. But the Almighty God is also mighty in love. He is a God of tenderness and mercy, a God always ready to grant pardon. When we reflect on the pardon of God, which is always offered, or rather on God who pardons, we make the strange discovery that this God is also a God of anger. His anger is directed toward those who are stubbornly proud and who do not admit that they are sinners. His pardon is for those who return to Him.

1. *The Teaching of the Qur'an*

bi-smi Llâhi l-raḥmâni l-raḥîm

We are very familiar with this invocation, which is found at the beginning of each *sûra* of the Qur'an, apart from *sûrat al-barâ'a* or *al-tawba,* "Repentance" (Q 9). It is nevertheless worth examining more closely.

From the root RḤM is derived the word *riḥm*, which means "the womb." This root, then, implies some connection with maternity, with a seat of affection that could be designated in the ancient biblical phrase "the bowels of mercy."

In the qur'anic invocation given above there are two words derived from this root: *raḥmân* and *raḥîm*, both used as Names for God.[1] The first of these words is a noun, in the augmentative form, which indicates the intensity of the quality designated by the root. Applied to God (and in fact it can be used for none other), it indicates that this quality belongs to God in the highest degree; we could say that it characterizes God. In fact, in South Arabic inscriptions from pre-Islamic times found in the Yemen, the word *raḥmânân* (where the suffix *ân* represents the definite article) is used for the Name of God in the Jewish tradition and for God the Father among the Christians.[2] Islam has tended to make abstraction of the paternal aspect, as well as the maternal aspect, of the root meaning, considering them to be unsuitable for attribution to God.

Raḥîm is adjectival, in a form that replaces the active participle. Here it qualifies God as giving expression to His *raḥma*.

But what exactly does *raḥma* mean? It is often translated as "mercy" or "compassion." The usual English translation of the invocation is thus "In the name of God the Merciful, the Compassionate." There are two drawbacks to this translation: first, it does not bring out that the two Names are derived from the same root, and second, that one of them is a noun and the other an adjective. Moreover *raḥma* does not really mean "mercy," but rather "tender-

[1] Cf. al-Ghazâlî, *The Ninety-Nine Beautiful Names*, pp. 52–57; Gimaret, *Les noms divins*, pp. 375–82; see also EQ, s.v. "*God and His Attributes.*"

[2] Cf. J. Jomier, "Le nom divin Al-Rahmân," in *Mélanges Louis Massignon* (Damas, France: Institut français de Damas, 1957).

ness," "kindness."[3] Inverting the two terms, one could say in English "the Good God of Goodness," or "the Bountiful God of Bounty." Abdel Haleem proposes "The Lord of Mercy, the Giver of Mercy."[4] *Al-raḥmân* is therefore one of the Names for God:

> Say [to them] "Call on God, or on the Lord of Mercy—*qul idʿû Llâha aw idʿû l-raḥmân*
>
> Whatever names you call Him, the best names belong to Him." (Q 17:110)

Allâh and *al-raḥmân* are thus presented in parallel fashion. *Al-raḥmân* was probably unknown in Mecca at the time of

---

[3] Cf. EI[2], s.v. "Rahma," where it is noted that the term does not really include the idea of forgiveness, although indulgence with regard to sinners can be considered an eminent form of kindness.

[4] Abdel Haleem explains his choice in two notes. "Most of the occurrences of this term *raḥmân* in the Qur'an are in the context of Him being mighty and majestic as well as merciful. The addition of the word 'Lord' here is intended to convey this aspect of the term. This term *raḥîm* is an intensive form suggesting that the quality of mercy is inherent in God's nature." Cf. *The Qur'an*, p. 2, nn. *a* and *b*.

Yusuf Ali has opted for "Most Gracious, Most Merciful." He explains: "The Arabic words . . . are both intensive forms referring to different aspects of God's attribute of Mercy. The Arabic intensive is more suited to express God's attributes than the superlative in English. The latter implies a comparison with other beings, or with other times or places, while there is no being like unto God, and He is independent of Time and Place. Mercy may imply pity, long-suffering, patience and forgiveness, all of which the sinner needs and God Most Merciful bestows in abundant measure. But there is a Mercy that goes before even the need arises, the Grace which is ever watchful, and flows from God Most Gracious to all his creatures, protecting them, preserving them, guiding them, and leading them to clearer light and higher life." Cf. *The Holy Qur'an*, p. 14, n. 19.

Muhammad, or at least may have been considered as a foreign god, hence the doubt regarding the use of this Name and the reassurance given by the Qur'an.

This Name appears in the Qur'an especially in the second Meccan period.[5] One of the *sûras* of the Second Meccan period is in fact called *al-raḥmân* (Q 55). It speaks of the gifts of God, starting with revelation and continuing with creation:

> It is the Lord of Mercy who taught the Qur'an. He created man and taught him to communicate. (Q 55:1-4).

After the mention of each wonder of creation comes the question:

> Which, then, of your Lord's blessings do you both deny?[6]

Sûrat al-rahmân is indeed a song of praise to God the Munificent.

Let us look now at the words derived from the root RḤM that occur in *sûrat maryam* (Q 19), which is of the same period.

---

[5] Muslims distinguish between the Meccan and the Medinan *sûras*. Orientalists have proposed a more precise division into different periods:

- First Meccan period (610–615): the initial preaching—a simple message with an eschatological dimension.
- Second Meccan period (615–619): the "biblical" period—stories from Scripture to support the message.
- Third Meccan period (619–622): confirmation in the face of opposition; divine omnipotence.
- Medinan period (622–632): the organization of the community: conflict, legislation.

Cf. R. Caspar, *A Historical Introduction to Islamic Theology: Muhammad and the Classical Period* (Rome: PISAI, 1998), pp. 26–27.

[6] The verb is in the dual form, understood as intending the jinn and humankind.

- This is an account of your Lord's grace (*raḥma*) towards His servant, Zechariah. (v. 2)
- She [Mary] said, "I seek the Lord of Mercy's protection (*aʿûdhu bi-l-raḥmân*) against you. (v. 18)
- We shall make him [Jesus] a sign to all people, a blessing (*raḥma*) from us. (v. 21)
- Say to anyone you may see: "I have vowed to the Lord of Mercy (*al-raḥmân*) to abstain from conversation, and I will not talk to anyone today." (v. 26)

(The Copts in Egypt still observe today what they call the Fast of the Virgin Mary, before the feast of the Dormition. Here in the text it is a question not of a fast from food, but from speaking; this reflects perhaps the monastic practice of silence.)

- When the revelations of the Lord of Mercy (*ayât al-raḥmân*, literally the "signs" or "verses" of the Lord of Mercy) were recited to them [the prophets], they fell to their knees and wept. (v. 58)
- They [the blessed] will enter the Gardens of Lasting Bliss, promised by the Lord of Mercy (*al-raḥmân*) to His servants. (v. 61)
- We shall seize out of each group those who were most disobedient towards the Lord of Mercy (*al-raḥmân*). (v. 69)
- Say [Prophet], "May the Lord of Mercy (*al-raḥmân*) lengthen [the lives] of the misguided. (v. 75)
- Has he penetrated the unknown or received a pledge to that effect from the Lord of Mercy (*al-raḥmân*)? (v. 78)
- On the Day We gather the righteous as an honored company (*wafd^an*—literally "as a delegation") before the Lord of Mercy

(*al-raḥmân*) . . . no one will have power to intercede except for those who have permission from the Lord of Mercy (*al-raḥmân*). (v. 87)

- The disbelievers say, "The Lord of Mercy (*al-raḥmân*) has offspring." (v .88)[7]
- They attribute offspring to the Lord of Mercy. (*al-raḥmân*) (v. 91)
- It does not befit the Lord of Mercy (*al-raḥmân*) [to have offspring]. (v. 92)
- There is no one in the heavens or earth who will not come to the Lord of Mercy (*al-raḥmân*) as a servant. (v. 93)
- But the Lord of Mercy (*al-raḥmân*) will give love (*wudd^{an}*) to those who believe and do righteous deeds. (v. 96)

The insistence on the Name al-raḥmân is striking. Verses 88-92 deny all possibility of generation in God. Note should be taken, all the same, of a mysterious verse addressed elsewhere to Muhammad:

Say [Prophet], If the Lord of Mercy [truly] had a son, I would be the first to worship him.[8]	*in kâna li-l-raḥmân walad^{un}*
(Q 43:81)	*fa-anâ awwalu l-ᶜâbidîn*

---

[7] Abdel Haleem remarks in a note here: "Many translators say 'a son' here, not realizing that *walad* in classical Arabic means 'child' or 'children.' The discussion here is about the pagans of Mecca, who said that angels were daughters of God."

[8] This is not the translation Abdel Haleem adopts, but one he gives in a note on the authority of Fakhr al-Dîn Râzî. The Arabic text uses the open conditional particle *in*, not the particle *law* used for a hypothetical condition, thus giving the impression that the possibility is real.

It is good to notice that Q 19:96 gives a very open definition of the just who will be rewarded by God, namely, the one who believes and who does righteous deeds. It is also worth noting that God will show love for the just. From this comes another Name for God, *al-wadûd*, the Loving or the Very Loving:[9]

> Ask forgiveness from your Lord, and turn to Him in repentance: my Lord is merciful and most loving. | *inna rabbî raḥîm wadûd*
> (Q 11:90)

Different interpretations are given for this Name. If it is considered to be the equivalent of an active participle, then it would refer to God loving his good servants, those who are near to Him, in other words, the saints (*al-awliyâ'*); in this sense God is the Friend of the Believers. The form can be taken, however, as an intensive, in which case it would be equivalent to saying God-Strong-in-Love. Nevertheless, it can also be understood as a passive, and so it would mean that God is the Loved One, the One who is loved by the believers, His good servants.

In general the commentators wish to avoid attributing love to God, especially when the term *ḥubb* is used, for they consider it as something that is too human and therefore not worthy of God. There are, however, two passages in the Qur'an in which it is said that God loves and in which words derived from the root ḤBB are used:

---

[9] Cf. al-Ghazâlî, *The Ninety-Nine Beautiful Names,* pp. 118–19, where this Name is translated "the Loving-kind." See also the final chapter of Gimaret's book, which concentrates on this Name, rendered as the "Friend of the Believers"; cf. *Les noms divins*, pp. 423–26.

> You who believe, if any of you go back on your faith, God will
> soon replace you with people He loves and who love Him.

| (Q 5:54) | *yuḥibbu-hum wa-yuḥibbûna-hu* |

It is interesting to see that God's love comes first, so it can be said
that the love of the believers is a response to divine love. Here
is the other text:

> Say, "If you love God,
>   follow me,   *in kuntum tuḥibbûna Llâha fa-ttabiᶜû-nî*
> and God will love you and forgive you
>   your sins;   *yuḥbib-kum Allâh*
> God is most forgiving,
>   most merciful.   *wa-Llâhu ghafûrun raḥîm*
>   (Q 3:31)

This brings us to another root, GH F R.[10]

Here also there is a *sûra* with the Name *al-ghâfir*, the Forgiver
(Q 40). Although this Name, which is found only once in the
Qur'an, does not figure as such in the list of Beautiful Names,
other forms that do figure in the list are frequent: *al-ghafûr*, the
Very Indulgent or the Oft-Forgiver (ninety-one times); *al-ghaffâr*,
the All-Forgiving (five times).

Here is the way the commentators distinguish the meaning
of these Names:

---

[10] Names derived from this root are considered in *Les noms divins*, pp.
409–13; see al-Ghazâlî, *The Ninety-Nine Beautiful Names*, pp. 100–101 for *al-ghafûr,* and pp. 73–74 for *al-ghaffâr*; see also EQ, s.v. "*God and his Attributes*,"
p. 321; and EI², s.v. "Ghufran."

al-ghâfir	the One who pardons a single sin;
al-ghafûr	the One who has a habit of pardoning sins;
al-ghaffâr	the One who never ceases to pardon; since

this noun-pattern is often used to indicate a profession, this Name could be translated "the Pardoner."

Yet I am most forgiving	*ghaffâr*
towards those who repent, believe,	
do righteous deeds, and stay on the right path. (Q 20:82)	

At the beginning of *sûrat al-ghâfir* there is the following passage:

This Scripture is sent down from God, the Almighty, the All-Knowing,	
Forgiver of sins and Accepter of repentance,	*ghâfir al-ḏanb qâbil al-tawb*
Severe in punishment, infinite in bounty. (Q 40:2-3)	*shadîd al-ʿiqâb dhî l-ṭawl*

What this teaches is obviously that it is necessary to hold together the two aspects of God: He will punish those who obstinately oppose His will, but He is also ready to pardon.

Let us return to the story of Moses, looking at it this time in *sûrat al-aʿrâf*, The Heights (Q 7). Moses has withdrawn in order to meet God on the mountain, leaving his brother Aaron in charge of the people. The people, however, demand a tangible god, and so they make for themselves "a mere shape that made sounds like a cow" (Q 7:148). Realizing that they have sinned, they say:

| "If our Lord does not have mercy on us | *la-ʾin lam yarḥam-nâ rabbu-nâ* |

And forgive us, we shall be losers."   *wa-yaghfir la-nâ*
   (Q 7:149)

Moses, "angry and aggrieved," throws down the tablets he has received and seizes his brother by the hair. But after his brother has complained, he prays:

"My Lord, forgive me and my brother; accept us into your mercy;
You are the Most Merciful of all who show mercy."
*rabbi ghfir lî wa-li-'akhî wa-dkhil-nâ fî raḥmati-ka wa-anta
   arḥamu l-râḥimîn*
   (Q 7: 151)

It is as if Moses wished his brother to be enfolded in the mercy of God.

A little further on the same sentiment is expressed in a different way:

"So forgive us and
   have mercy on us.   *fa-'aghfir la-nâ wa-rḥamnâ*
You are the best of
   those who forgive."   *wa-anta khayru l-ghâfirîn*
   (Q 7:155)

This God who forgives is also the One who turns ceaselessly (*al-tawwâb*) to his creatures and is therefore the source of all repentance (*tawba*).[11]

As for those who hide the proofs and guidance We send down,
   after We have made them clear to people in the Scripture, God

---

[11] On this Name see al-Ghazâlî, *The Ninety-Nine Beautiful Names*, pp. 137–38, and Gimaret, *Les noms divins*, pp. 416-18; see also EI², "Tawwâb," where it is noted that the Name *al-tawwâb* is found exclusively in the Medinan *sûras*. The word *tawba* in Arabic is equivalent to *shubh* in Hebrew.

rejects them, and so do others, unless they repent, make amends and declare the truth. I will certainly accept their repentance: I am the Ever Relenting, the Most Merciful. *fa-ʿulâʾika atûbu ʿalay-him wa-anâ al-tawwâb al-raḥîm* (Q 2:159-160)

One of the names for *sûra* 9 is *al-tawba*, "Repentance," and a passage from this *sûra* deals with this theme. It speaks of the Arabs, that is, the inhabitants of the desert, the Bedouins (Abdel Haleem in fact translates "desert Arabs"). It is not sure whether their conversion is sincere, for they are said to be "the most stubborn of all people in their disbelief" (*ashaddu kufran*, Q 9:97). They find burdensome the financial obligations of the religion they have adopted. Some of them, however, are true believers: they "consider their contributions as bringing them nearer to God" (v. 99). Toward them God is merciful:

God will admit them to His mercy.	*sa-yudkhilu-hum Allâhu fî raḥmati-hi*
God is forgiving and merciful. (Q 9:99)	*inna Llâha ghafûrun raḥîm.*

Among them there are also some hypocrites (*munâfiqûn*) who will be punished. Others recognize their faults and so may obtain pardon:

And there are others who have confessed their wrongdoing, who have done some righteous deeds and some bad ones: God may well accept their repentance, for God is most forgiving and merciful. *ʿasâ Llâhu an yatûba ʿalay-him inna Llâha ghafûrun raḥîm* (Q 9: 102)

The passage ends with a general declaration:

Do they not know that it is God Himself who accepts repentance from His servants and receives what is given freely for His sake? He is always ready to accept repentance, most merciful, *al-tawwâb al-rahîm.*   (Q 9:104).

2. *In the OT*

It is often in the Psalms that we find expressed faith in a God of bountiful mercy. Here are just a few examples. Psalm 136 begins:

O give thanks to the LORD, for he is good,
    for his steadfast love endures forever. (Ps 136 [135]:1)

This psalm celebrates the goodness of God, manifested in the first place through creation and then in the history of the chosen people. The opening verse is repeated again at the end of the psalm, as if to underline God's faithfulness.

Another psalm, Psalm 103, also acclaims the goodness of the Lord.

Bless the LORD, O my soul,
    and all that is within me,
    bless his holy name.
Bless the LORD, O my soul,
    and do not forget all his benefits. (Ps 103 [102]:1-2)

What are these benefits? There is forgiveness and healing. There is the gift of fidelity and of tenderness, a share, one could say, in qualities that are found in an eminent way in God.

[The God] who forgives all your iniquity,
    who heals all your diseases,
who redeems your life from the Pit,
    who crowns you with steadfast love and with mercy. (vv. 3-4)

This divine goodness is source of life:

> who satisfies you with good as long as you live
>> so that your youth is renewed like the eagle's. (v. 5)

And then:

> The LORD is merciful and gracious,
>> slow to anger and abounding in steadfast love. (v. 8)

> As a father has compassion for his children,
> So the LORD has compassion for those who fear him (v. 13)

There is a vast difference between this eternal God and created beings that are like dust. Mortal beings are like grass that flourishes one day and then dies, whereas the faithfulness of the Lord endures forever (cf. vv. 15-17).

Here is another example:

> O give thanks to the LORD, for he is good;
>> for his steadfast love endures forever. (Ps 107 [106]:1)

God's merciful love (*ḥesed* in Hebrew[12]) is eternal, yet God does not cease to show this love to those who cry to Him in their distress (cf. vv. 6, 13, 19, 28).

---

[12] Cf. ABD, s.v. "Love." Hebrew has several words with which to express the idea of love: *dôd*, used of a man loved by a woman in a relationship normally destined to be crowned by marriage; *ra'ya*, said of a woman loved by a man in a similar type of relationship to that just stated; *yadîd*, applied normally to Israel, or a section of Israel, as the object of God's love; *hashaq*, the desire for a permanent attachment (akin to the Arabic *'ishq*, which indicates passionate love); *'âhêb*, loving friendship, which can be either negative (possessive love) or positive, and is used to describe the love that humans have for God; *ḥesed*, tender, faithful love, and mercy.

God is merciful. This in fact is God's own self-definition given during the theophany described in the book of Exodus:

> The Lord descended in the cloud and stood with him [Moses] there, and proclaimed the name "the Lord." The Lord passed before him and proclaimed:
> "The Lord, the Lord,
> a God merciful and gracious,
> slow to anger,
> and abounding in steadfast love and faithfulness,
> keeping steadfast love for the thousandth generation,
> forgiving iniquity and transgression and sin,
> yet by no means clearing the guilty,
> but visiting the iniquity of the parents
> upon the children
> and the children's children,
> to the third and the fourth generation." (Exod 34:5-7)

The prophet Hosea gives a daring portrait of this God of tenderness. He describes a love that is paternal:

> When Israel was a child, I loved him,
>   and out of Egypt I called my son. (Hos 11:1)

Going back over its history, the people can call to mind how God led them like a small child. Yet, this is also a history of misunderstanding on the people's part:

> . . . but they did not know that I healed them. (v. 3)

One can feel the divine disappointment:

> My people are bent on turning away from me. (v. 7)

What is God's reaction? It is revealed as being one of patience and tenderness that could be qualified as paternal or even maternal:

How can I give you up, Ephraim?
>How can I hand you over, O Israel?

. . .

My heart recoils within me;
>my compassion grows warm and tender.

I will not execute my fierce anger;
>I will not again destroy Ephraim;

for I am God and no mortal,
>the Holy One in your midst,
>and I will not come in wrath. (Hos 11:8-9)

Can it be said that God is a mother for us? It has already been seen how, in the Canticle of the Rock of Israel in Deuteronomy, the author contrasts the faithfulness of the Rock with the lack of faithfulness of the people.

He abandoned God who made him,
>and scoffed at the Rock of his salvation.

. . .

You were unmindful of the Rock that bore you;[13]
>you forgot the God who gave you birth. (Deut 32:15, 18)

If to beget is the function of the father, to give birth is certainly the role of the mother.

Moses is conscious of this maternal responsibility of God. The Book of Numbers presents us with a drama in which three actors are involved: God, the people, and Moses.

One day, to the Lord's displeasure, the people started complaining about their misfortunes in the Lord's hearing. The Lord's anger was kindled when he heard them. Fire came down upon the people

---

[13] An alternative reading is "that begot you."

and burned some parts of the camp. The people cried out to Moses to intercede with the Lord for them, and the fire abated (Num 11:1-2). But the people were never satisfied: they had asked for food, but the manna God gave was not enough; they craved meat.

> Then the Lord became very angry, and Moses was displeased. So Moses said to the Lord: "Why have you treated your servant so badly? Why have I not found favor in your sight, that you lay the burden of all this people on me? Did I conceive all this people? Did I give birth to them, that you should say to me: 'Carry them in your bosom, as a nurse carries a sucking child,' to the land that you promised on oath to their ancestors?" (Num 11:11-12)

This duty to lead the people to the Promised Land, considered a maternal duty, lies heavily on Moses, but he will share it with others. We are not alone in carrying the mission that the Lord entrusts to us.

3. *The NT*[14]

The God merciful and gracious; this is the divine self-definition of God given to Moses. In the First Letter of John we find another definition:

> Beloved, let us love one another, because love is from God; everyone who loves is born of God and knows God. Whoever does not love does not know God, for God is love. (1 John 4:7-8)

It is useful to continue the quotation:

---

[14] Cf. ABD, s.v. "Love."

> God's love was revealed among us in this way: God sent his only
> Son into the world so that we might live through him. In this is
> love, not that we loved God but that he loved us and sent his Son
> to be the atoning sacrifice for our sins. Beloved, since God loved
> us so much, we also ought to love one another. (1 John 4:9-11)

We are invited to assimilate the qualities designated by the Names
of God. If, therefore, God is love, then love should characterize
our relations with our brothers and sisters.

Out of love, God is merciful. It is above all the Gospel of Luke
that insists on the mercy of God. We find there, in chapter 15,
the three parables about divine mercy, but we can also discover
the tenderness of Jesus.

> As he [Jesus] came near and saw the city [Jerusalem], he wept
> over it, saying, "If you, even you, had only recognized on this day
> the things that make for peace! But now they are hidden from
> your eyes." (Luke 19:41)

In weeping over this city that does not want to receive his message of salvation, Jesus shows his love for the Holy City. Yet, we
may ask: how efficacious are these tears? Jesus wept for his friend
Lazarus (cf. John 11:35), but on that occasion his compassion led
him to raise Lazarus from the dead. Here it is to his passion that
his tears will lead, and to a death outside the city, but both for
the city itself and for the multitude.

Jesus had already lamented over Jerusalem:

> Jerusalem, Jerusalem, the city that kills the prophets and stones
> those who are sent to it! How often have I desired to gather your
> children together as a hen gathers her brood under her wings,
> and you were not willing! (Luke 13:34)

Jesus wished to gather, to bring into unity, but, like the prophets before him, he met with opposition. He will not be saved miraculously from the hands of those who are seeking his death. He does not try to escape. On the contrary, he moves forward with open eyes. He is in solidarity with all those who suffer for the sake of justice. He knows what is going to happen to him. He has foretold it:

> The Son of Man must undergo great suffering and be rejected
> by the elders, chief priests and scribes, and be killed, and on the
> third day be raised. (Luke 9:22)

We could say that meditation on the tenderness of God, crystallized in Jesus, necessarily opens up the perspective of the Cross.

As Christians we are called to share in the merciful tenderness of the Lord:

> Be merciful, just as your Father is merciful. (Luke 6:36)

This is Luke's version of the command found in Matthew: "Be perfect, therefore, as your heavenly Father is perfect" (Matt 5:48). How are we to be merciful? we may ask. How are we to be perfect? Luke continues:

> Do not judge, and you will not be judged; do not condemn, and
> you will not be condemned. (Luke 6:37)

We may remember the saying *al-ḥukm li-Llâh*: judgment belongs to God. As Matthew explains in conjunction with the prayer that Jesus has taught us, our pardon is linked to that coming from the Father. If we pardon, then we shall be granted pardon. But we could also say, with St. Paul, that we must ourselves pardon others precisely because we have received the Lord's pardon:

As God's chosen ones, holy and beloved, clothe yourselves with compassion, kindness, meekness, and patience. Bear with one another and, if anyone has a complaint against another, forgive each other; just as the Lord has forgiven you, so you also must forgive. Above all, clothe yourselves with love, which binds everything together in perfect harmony. And let the peace of Christ rule in your hearts, to which you were called in the one body. And be thankful. (Col 3:12-15)

Pardon, received and given, is an essential element of our Christian witness.

All this is from God, who reconciled us to himself through Christ, and has given us the ministry of reconciliation; that is, in Christ God was reconciling the world to himself, not counting their trespasses against them, and entrusting the message of reconciliation to us. So we are ambassadors for Christ, since God is making his appeal through us: we entreat you on behalf of Christ, be reconciled to God. (2 Cor 5:18-20)

V

God, Lord and King

The pendulum swings once more between the immanence and the transcendence of God. From the God of tenderness and goodness we turn to the God of majesty, the Lord and King.

1. *The Teaching of the Qur'an*

Several of the Names of God emphasize divine power. There is first of all *al-qahhâr*,[1] the Dominator, or the All Powerful, which is found six times in the Qur'an together with *al-wâhid*, the One, or the Unique. These Names are found together in the story of Joseph.

Joseph, having been unjustly accused of trying to seduce the mistress of the house, is thrown into prison. There he says to his fellow prisoners:

"Would many diverse gods be better than God the One, the All Powerful?" (Q 12:39)	*Allâh al-wâhid al-qahhâr*

Another text takes up the same idea:

---

[1] Cf. al-Ghazâlî, *The Ninety-Nine Beautiful Names*, p. 74.

Have the partners they assign to God created anything like His creation so that their creation is indistinguishable from His? Say, "God is the Creator of all things: He is the One, the All Compelling." (Q 13:16)

The root QHR conveys the idea of the power to conquer, with a hint at the use of force, of coercion (from it is derived *al-qâhira*, the Victorious, the city built by the Fatimids, from which we get Cairo, the name of the present-day capital of Egypt). Gimaret explains how the Muslim commentators understood the application of this idea to God: "God's domination is understood in two ways. It has a universal meaning in so far as God 'dominates all His creatures, governing them as He wills, bringing them life, death, suffering, etc., without their being able to oppose His will. . . .' But there is also a particular sense, in so far as God overcomes and humiliates the powers of this world."[2]

The fact that the Name *al-qahhâr* is combined with that of *al-wâhid* is quite significant. There is no room for dualism in Islam; there cannot exist side by side a principle of good and a principle of evil, as in the ancient religions of Persia, Mazdaism, or Zoroastrianism, which were known at the time of Islam's birth. The power of God and God's uniqueness are underlined at the same time.

al-jabbâr[3]

This word is used in the Qur'an with its ordinary meaning of "tyrant."

These were the 'Ad: they rejected their Lord's signs, disobeyed His messengers, and followed the command of every obstinate tyrant. (Q 11:59)

---

[2] Gimaret, *Les noms divins*, pp. 241–42.
[3] Cf. al-Ghazâlî, *The Ninety-Nine Beautiful Names*, pp. 66–67.

Yet it is applied to God also:

> He is God: there is no god other
>   than Him,
> the Controller, the Holy One,
>   the Source of Peace,
> Granter of Security,
>   Guardian over all, the Almighty,
> the Compellor, the Truly Great.   *al-jabbâr al-mutakabbir*[4]
>   (Q 59:23)

Using this Name is one way of stressing that God is invincible. Nevertheless, the note of violence attached to it can create some uneasiness. This encourages the suggestion of a different etymology. The Name would be derived from *jabara*, which means to repair or restore something to its original state. *Jabr* is the term used for a splint applied to a fractured limb. The one who applies this remedy is thus *al-jabbâr*, the Healer. God, therefore, is the One who returns human beings to their proper state, from the misfortune of evil to the happiness brought by righteousness.

Let us now examine the Name "King," *al-malik*.[5] It occurred in the passage just quoted where it was translated Controller. Yusuf Ali prefers Sovereign. This Name is found over forty times in the Qur'an, for instance in the very last *sûra*:

---

[4] The last-mentioned Name, *al-mutakabbir*, the Haughty, is considered by Gimaret in the chapter entitled "Parfait"; see *Les noms divins*, pp. 212–13. See also al-Ghazâlî, *The Ninety-Nine Beautiful Names*, p. 67, where the Name is translated as "the Proud." Some commentators take it simply as an equivalent of *kabîr*, the Great, but others, such as Ghazâlî and Fakhr al-Dîn Râzî, accept that pride, blameworthy for creatures, can legitimately be attributed to God.

[5] Cf. al-Ghazâlî, *The Ninety-Nine Beautiful Names,* pp. 57–59; Gimaret, *Les noms divins*, chap. 16, "Souverain," pp. 313–26; see also EI², s.vv. " Malik" and "Mulk"; also EQ, s.v. "Kings and Rulers."

Say, "I seek refuge with the Lord of people,
> the King[6] of people,   *malik al-nâs*
the God of people, against the harm of the slinking whisperer—
who whispers into the hearts of people—
whether they be jinn or people." (Q 114:1-6)

God is the powerful ruler or king who can deliver us from evil, or from the Evil One. Christians, in the prayer that Jesus taught his disciples, the Our Father, also ask to be delivered from the Evil One.[7]

To God belongs all sovereignty, according to the *sûra* that bears this name, *sûrat al-mulk*, Sovereignty (Q 67).[8] It begins:

Exalted is He who holds
> all control in His hands;   *tabâraka lladhî bi-yadi-hi l-mulk*
Who has power over all things. (Q 67:1)

Elsewhere we find:

Say, "O God, Lord of Power (and Rule)   *mâlik al-mulk*
You give power to whoever you will
and remove it from whoever you will;
You elevate whoever You will and humble whoever You will.
All that is good lies in Your hand;
You have power over everything." (Q 3:26)[9]

We can understand from these texts that to God alone belongs "royal power" (*mulk*), though He can share this power with

---

[6] Abdel Haleem gives this translation in a note, as well as another alternative, "Master." He adopts for his own translation "Controller."

[7] Cf. Matt 6:13: "from the evil one" is the reading preferred by the NRSV and the JB, as well as by the *Traduction Oecuménique de la Bible*, although "from evil," as in the traditional prayer formula, is acceptable.

[8] This is the name given in a note by Abdel Haleem; in his text he has "Control." Yusuf Ali prefers "Dominion."

[9] Translation modified following the version of Yusuf Ali.

whomsoever He wills. The Qur'an therefore acknowledges the existence of earthly rulers, such as Pharaoh and Saul. Yet, Islam is presenting a new order in which God alone is the real king.

Everything, as we see, belongs to God. He is the One who elevates or grants honor (*al-muʿizz*), as He is the One who brings low or humbles (*al-mudhill*), as He wills. Something similar is found in the Song of Mary, the Magnificat, where it is said of God that "He has brought down the mighty from their thrones and has lifted up the lowly" (Luke 1:52).

Islam emphasizes the primacy of divine will. God is always the Sovereign Master. This is so firmly fixed in the minds of Muslims that they find difficulty with the Our Father that Christians recite so often. How can one say to God: "Your kingdom come, your will be done"? God's will surely comes about necessarily, they say. It is for Christians to explain that God endows human beings with liberty, and that they are free to respond or not to respond to His invitation, to do His will or to refuse to obey it.

There is another Name, one that is not found among the ninety-nine but that is constantly used, and that is Lord (*al-rabb*).[10] This Name is encountered in the very first passage of the Qur'an chronologically speaking:

> Proclaim! In the name of your Lord
>   who created.　　　　　　　　　*iqra' bi-smi rabbi-ka*
>   (Q 96:1)[11]

---

[10] Gimaret notes that in fact this Name never appears with the definite article, but always in a construct state, as can be seen from the examples given; cf. *Les noms divins*, p. 318. On this Name see also EI², s.v. "Rabb"; see, too, EQ, s.v. "*God and His Attributes*," pp. 318–19.

[11] Translation modified following the version of Yusuf Ali.

It appears also in the *Fâtiḥa*, the opening *sûra*:

> Praise belongs to God;
>> Lord of the Worlds.   *rabb al-ʿâlamîn*
>> (Q 1:2)

In the first text, which is addressed directly to Muhammad, note should be taken of the personal relationship that it marks: *rabbi-ka*, your Lord. On the other hand, in the *Fâtiḥa* the emphasis is on the universality of the lordship of God: *rabb al-ʿâlamîn*. God is the Lord of the Worlds, in other words, of all things.

There is an interesting use of this Name in the story of Moses and Pharaoh. God says to Moses:

> Go, both of you, to Pharaoh and say, "We bring a message from the Lord of the Worlds: let the Children of Israel leave with us."
> (Q 26:16-17)

Moses is sent together with his brother Aaron, who is to act as his spokesperson. They are, in fact, designated as forming one single messenger: *innâ rasûlu rabbi l-ʿâlamîn*, literally, "Indeed we are a messenger of the Lord of the Worlds."

> Pharaoh said,
> "Did we not bring you up
>> as a child among us?   *a-lam nurabbi-ka fî-nâ walîdan*
> Did you not stay with us for many years?
> And then you committed that crime of yours:
> you were so ungrateful." (Q 26:18-19)

The crime referred to is the killing by Moses of an Egyptian who was beating a Hebrew. This event is not otherwise mentioned in this *sûra*, but an allusion is made to it in *sûra Ṭâ Hâ* (Q 20:40). In order to understand the reaction of Pharaoh, who treats Moses as one who is ungrateful, attention needs to be paid to the verb used, *rabbâ*, from the root RBY. The roots RBB and RBY are very close, the second meaning "to bring up a child." As Abdel Haleem says in a note to his translation of the *Fâtiḥa*, "The Arabic root *r-b-b* has connotations of caring and nurturing in addition to lordship, and this should be borne in mind wherever the term occurs and is rendered 'lord.'"[12] God, the Lord, is also an educator, and Pharaoh claims this title for himself.

Pharaoh asked, "What is this 'Lord of the Worlds'?"	*wa-mâ rabb al-ʿâlamîn*
Moses replied, "He is the Lord of the heavens and earth	*rabb al-samawâti wa-l-ʿarḍ*
And everything between them." (Q 26:23-34)	

So God is the Lord of all that exists in space.

"He is your Lord and the Lord of your Forefathers	*rabbu-kum*
	wa-rabbu
(Q 26:26)	*abâ'i-kum al-ʿawwalîn*

He is the Lord of all time, of history.

| Lord of the East and West and everything between them. (Q 26:28) | *rabb al-mashriq wa-l-maghrib* |

He is the Lord of all variety in creation.
   Pharaoh, however, refuses this message:

[12] Cf. *The Qur'an*, p. 2, n. *d.* See also Gimaret, *Les noms divins*, p. 319.

Pharaoh said, "If you take any other god but me, I will throw
you into prison."
(Q 26:29)

Moses works signs, and the court magicians are convinced by
them:

The sorcerers fell down on their knees, exclaiming,
"We believe in the Lord
   of the Worlds,   *âmannâ bi-rabb al-ʿâlamîn*
the Lord of Moses and Aaron."   *rabbi mûsa wa-hârûn*
   (Q 26:46-48)

This God then becomes their Lord, because to Pharaoh who is
threatening them they reply:

"That will do us no harm,
for we are sure to return
   to our Lord.   *ilâ rabbi-nâ munqalibûn*
We hope that our Lord will forgive us our sins,
as we were the first to believe." (Q 26:50-51)

Later on, Moses declares his faith before the people, who are full
of fear, since they are pursued by Pharaoh and his army:

Moses said, "No, my Lord
   is with me: *inna maʿiya rabbî*
He will guide me." (Q 26:62)

This whole passage relating the story of Moses ends with a refrain,
echoing an earlier verse:

Your Lord alone is the Almighty,   *wa-inna rabba-ka*
   the Merciful.   *la-huwa l-ʿazîz al-raḥîm*
      (Q 26:68; cf. Q 26:9)

If the normal attitude before the Lord is that of the adoring servant (*ʿabd*), given the fact that the Lord, *al-rabb*, is also the Educator, *al-murabbî*, or the Nourisher, there can also be present an attitude of filial trust. The servant will be ready to obey, to speak, to give witness, to suffer, with the assurance of the Lord's presence and assistance.

2. *The OT*

The Kingship of God[13] is very present in the OT, particularly in the Psalms. The group of psalms known as "the Psalms of the Kingship of God" (Pss 93 [92]; 96 [95]–99 [98]) celebrate with enthusiasm God who sits upon His throne, who is king and judge of Israel, but who is also the master of the nations. Although they derive their origin from local coronation ceremonies, they are universalistic in their outlook. The present that they celebrate actualizes the past and anticipates the future. "The liturgy makes the past relive and revives hope."[14]

> The Lord is king, he is robed in majesty. (Ps 93 [92]:1)

This acclamation evokes another of the ninety-nine Names of God: *dhû l-jalâl wa-l-ikrâm*, the One endowed with Majesty and Generosity.

> Majestic on high is the Lord. (Ps 93 [92]:4)

This may recall also the Name *al-mutakabbir*, the Haughty.

---

[13] Cf. ABD, s.v. "King and Kingship," and in particular the section on YHWH as King, pp. 43–44; see also ABD, s.vv. "Kingdom of God," "Kingdom of Heaven."

[14] *Traduction Oecuménique de la Bible*, Introduction to the Psalms, p. 1262.

Psalm 96 [95] is a hymn to the magnificence of God in which He is proclaimed great, revered, and his splendor and majesty are praised.

Psalm 99 [98] exalts the King who makes peoples tremble. His Name is great and awesome. He is holy, one who loves justice and establishes equity. Worship is His due:

> Extol the LORD our God,
>> and worship at his holy mountain;
>> for the LORD our God is holy (Ps 99 [98]:9)

As has been noted, these psalms were composed originally for enthronement ceremonies of earthly kings. It was not without difficulty that Israel adopted the institution of kingship. The people of Israel were ruled by judges until the time of Samuel. The Scripture relates that when Samuel became old, "he made his sons judges over Israel" (1 Sam 8:1). The question may be asked whether inherited power is a good thing. As the text notes: "Yet his sons did not follow in his ways, but turned aside after gain; they took bribes and perverted justice" (1 Sam 8:3). In any case, the people demanded to have a king; they wanted to be like the nations around them.

> Then all the elders gathered together and came to Samuel at Ramah, and said to him, "You are old and your sons do not follow in your ways; appoint for us, then, a king to govern us, like other nations." (1 Sam 8:4)

Samuel was not pleased, but he interceded for the people before the Lord, and the Lord replied:

> Listen to the voice of the people in all that they say to you; for they have not rejected you, but they have rejected me from being king over them. (1 Sam 8:7)

Moreover, God tells Samuel to warn the people of the inconveniences of having a temporal king. This Samuel does, but the people insist:

> No, but we are determined to have a king over us, so that we also may be like other nations, and that our king may govern us and go out before us and fight our battles. (1 Sam 8:19-20)

So God said to Samuel:

> Listen to their voice and set a king over them. (1 Sam 8:22)

What the people are refusing is their special vocation as a people depending directly on God. They wish to be no different from other nations. The Lord accepts this; He allows the institution of kingship to be set up, and in fact He draws good out of it. He guides Samuel to the choice of David, of whose descent will come the Messiah who will be a King of a quite different kind.

As regards the Name "Lord," it is the usual name for God in the OT, replacing as it does the tetragram YHWH.[15] So we find it in the Psalms coupled with the Name "King." Here is another example of the use of this Name:

> Praise the LORD!
> Praise, O servants of the LORD;
>   praise the name of the LORD.
> Blessed be the name of the LORD
>   from this time on and for evermore.

[15] Cf. ABD, s.v. "Names of God." The name *'adôn*, more often found in the form *'adonai*, indicates a relationship that is not that of property (as does *ba'al*), but of authority; its antonym is *'ebêd*, subordinate, servant, or slave. See also ABD, s.vv. "Adonai," "Kingdom of God," "Kingdom of Heaven."

> From the rising of the sun to its setting
>> the name of the Lord is to be praised.
>
> . . .
>
> Who is like the LORD our God,
>> who is seated on high . . . ?
> He raises the poor from the dust,
>> and lifts the needy from the ash heap. (Ps 113 [112]:1-3, 5, 7)

The Lord reigns from on high; there is none like Him; yet He is good to the poor.

2. *The NT*

Jesus made a distinction between an earthly king and the King of heaven when he declared:

> Give therefore to the emperor the things that are the emperor's, and to God the things that are God's. (Matt 22:21)

In his time people were well aware of what earthly kings were like; they were familiar with the domination of the Roman emperor, and with the cruelty of a King Herod. Jesus warned his disciples:

> You know that among the Gentiles those whom they recognize as their rulers lord it over them, and their great ones are tyrants over them. But it is not so among you: but whoever wishes to become great among you must be your servant, and whoever wishes to be first among you must be slave of all. For the Son of Man came not to be served but to serve, and to give his life as a ransom for many. (Mark 10:42-45).

Jesus is our model. He is the king of the Jews, born in Bethlehem, whom the Magi came to adore, but whom Herod wished to eliminate.

Jesus, the king who was driven into exile, will return to live among his people, humble and hidden.

It is, we may say, especially through the passion that the true kingship of Jesus appears. He is delivered by the High Priest and the Sanhedrin to the Governor, Pontius Pilate. Pilate interrogates Jesus:

> "Are you the King of the Jews?" . . . Jesus answered, "My kingdom is not from this world." (John 18:33, 36)

Jesus did not come into this world to exercise domination. He will not use force to escape from his lot; he will not appeal for the help of angelic forces. All he desires is to render witness to the truth.

Pilate offers to the crowd the possibility of having released to them "the King of the Jews," but they call for the release of Barabbas. Jesus is rejected; he is not accepted as King of the Jews. This perhaps conforms to the truth, for Jesus, in spite of the inscription appended to the Cross, is not really the King of the Jews. He cannot be the king of a single people; he is the universal King, the one who has given his life for the multitude.[16]

Jesus is mocked as a king by the soldiers. Presented once more to the crowd, he is given another name: *Ecce homo*—"Here is the man" (John 19:5). Jesus is at this moment united with every person who is despised or oppressed. He is in solidarity with those who are without rights, who remain nameless, just ciphers.

Pilate gives the title of king to Jesus, but the High Priests will have none of it: "We have no king but the emperor" (John 19:15).

It is on the cross that the kingship of Jesus becomes manifest. He had said beforehand: "And I, when I am lifted up from the

---

[16] For a commentary on this passage of John's Gospel see Francis J. Moloney, *The Gospel of John*, pp. 494–95.

earth, will draw all people to myself" (John 12:32). This very special way of being king—through the gift of himself, through the gift of his life—Jesus had announced during the paschal meal with his disciples. He washed their feet and then explained:

> Do you know what I have done to you? You call me Teacher and Lord—and you are right, for that is what I am. So if I, your Lord and Teacher, have washed your feet, you also ought to wash one another's feet. For I have set you an example, that you should also do what I have done to you. (John 13:12-15)

We see that Jesus accepts to be called Lord. In the NT the title Lord (*kyrios*) is given to Jesus expressing faith in his divinity. Peter proclaims to the assembled people on the day of Pentecost:

> God has made him both Lord and Messiah, this Jesus whom you crucified. (Acts 2:36)

The one who was "declared to be Son of God with power according to the spirit of holiness by resurrection from the dead" can be called "Jesus Christ our Lord" (Rom 1:3). This is the Christian profession of faith; it is our *shahâda*. "No one can say 'Jesus is Lord' except by the Holy Spirit" (1 Cor 12:3).

Baptism seals this faith and inserts us into the community of faith. If we have been baptized as children, this incorporation into Jesus and into his Body will be confirmed, ratified, made personal by an act of faith that is continually renewed.

We are called to have a personal attachment to Jesus, our Lord and King. We are to allow Jesus to be the Lord of our lives, of the whole of our lives, without *shirk*, that is, avoiding associating anything with him, not trying to serve two masters at the same time, but giving ourselves wholly to our Lord.

VI

God the Guide

We are called to serve our King. Disciples of Jesus, we have accepted to follow him. We must continue along the road, but often we ask ourselves what we are to do. The more we advance along this road, the more we feel the need of a guide. In fact, it is God who is our guide. As in the past He led His people, so today He leads us. In His light we see the light.

1. *The Teaching of the Qur'an*

One of the Beautiful Names of God is *al-hâdî*,[1] the Guide. We can easily understand the importance of this role in the desert, where the tracks are often difficult to find and to follow.

---

[1] Gimaret examines this Name in the chapter entitled "Guide," together with *al-rashîd,* the Leader, *al-mubîn*, the Evident, or the One who makes all things clear, *al-burhân*, the Proof, or the one who affords the Proof, *al-nûr,* Light; cf. *Les noms divins*, pp. 367–74. Only the first and the last of the Names mentioned will be taken into account here. On *al-hâdî* see al-Ghazâlî, *The Ninety-Nine Beautiful Names*, pp. 145–46.

In fact, this Name is not found as such in the Qur'an, except for this verse:

God guides the faithful to the straight path. (Q 22:54)	*Inna Llâha hâdî lladhîna âmanû ilâ ṣirâṭ al-mustaqîm*

The active participle *hâdî* has been translated here by a verb. If one were to give a literal translation it would be: "In truth, God is guiding (or One who guides) those who have believed to the straight path," a translation that would bring out more clearly the basis for this divine Name.

The idea of divine guidance is well anchored in the minds of Muslims by this petition in the *Fâtiḥa*:

Guide us to the straight path. (Q 1:6)	*ihdi-nâ ṣirâṭ al-mustaqîm.*

To understand more fully what this means, we can take again the passage of the Qur'an that describes how Abraham arrived at the true faith (cf. Q 6:75-90). He is tempted to give worship to the astral bodies, but first the star that he has seen disappears, and then the moon. This leads Abraham to cry out:

"If my Lord does not guide me, I shall be one of those who go astray." (Q 6:77)	*la-'in lam yahdi-nî rabbî la-akûnanna min al-qawm al-ḍâllîn*

This realization does not prevent Abraham from wishing to give worship to the sun, but when the sun disappears likewise, he professes his faith in the One God. To his people who oppose him, he replies:

How can you argue with me about God when He has guided me?	*wa-qad hâda-nî*

We can see from this that the guidance given by God is a source of security.

It is those who have faith, and do not mix their faith with idolatry,[2] who will be secure and it is they who are rightly guided. (Q 6:82)	*la-hum al-ʿamn* *wa-hum muhtadîn*

It must be remembered that "faith" and "security" both come from the same root 'MN.

Furthermore, it is made clear that the descendants of Abraham are guided, as were those of Noah and, among his descendants, David, Solomon, Job, Joseph, Moses, Zechariah, John, Jesus, Elijah, Ishmael, Elisha, Jonah, and Lot (cf. Q 6:84-86). This list may seem somewhat confused; it certainly does not follow any chronological order. What is important, however, is the declaration that follows:

We chose them and guided them on a straight path. Such is God's guidance: with it He guides whoever of His servants He will. (Q 6:87-88)	*wa-hadaynâ-hum* *dhâlika hudâ Llâh*

---

[2] Yusuf Ali has "and confuse not their beliefs with wrong"; the term used, *zulm*, means wrong, injustice, oppression.

Consequently,

Those were the people
    God guided.
[Prophet], follow the guidance
    they received.
      (Q 6:90)
	ulâ'ika lladhîna hâda Llâh
	
	fa-bi-hudâ-hum uqtadih

Perhaps the Nestorian Patriarch Timothy was not mistaken, when Caliph al-Ma'mûn asked him to give his opinion on Muhammad as prophet, to answer: "He walked in the footsteps of the prophets."[3]

This divine guidance (*hudâ*) is felt particularly in time of difficulty, in the midst of dangers. We have already noted the verse of the Qur'an in which Moses expresses his confidence in God, at that very moment when it seemed certain that the army of Pharaoh would overtake the people of Israel:

"No, my Lord is with me:
    He will guide me."
      (Q 26:62)
	kallâ inna maʿiya rabbî sa-yahdî-nî

According to the constant pattern of qur'anic teaching, all prophets meet with opposition, and then God saves them from danger. This pattern is expressed in a general principle:

We have always appointed adversaries from the wicked,
    for every prophet:

---

[3] On the dialogue of Timothy with al-Ma'mûn, see J. M. Gaudeul, *Encounters and Clashes: Islam and Christianity in History* (Rome: Pontifical Institute of Arabic and Islamic Studies, 2000), vol. 1: *A Survey*, 36–38; vol. 2: *Texts*, 248–52.

Your Lord is sufficient
   guide and helper.   *wa-kafâ bi-rabbi-ka hâdiy^{an} wa-naṣîr^{an}*
   (Q25:31)

But opposition does not come only from the outside; it may arise in the very heart of the messenger of God:

We have never sent any messenger or prophet before you [Muhammad] into whose wishes Satan did not insinuate something. (Q 22:52)

The best-known example of such temptation is the episode of the "satanic verses." *Sûrat al-najm*, "The Star" (Q 53) refers to the goddesses worshipped by the Meccans:

[Disbelievers], consider al-Lat and al-'Uzza, and the third, other one, Manat. (Q 53:19-20)

According to the accounts given in the Qur'an commentaries, Muhammad continued: "They are the cranes on whose intercession one can rely." The cranes, elegant birds, represented the exalted goddesses. What was being proclaimed, therefore, was a compromise with a form of polytheism in order to win over the Meccans. This, however, was not to be. God, or the angel, showed Muhammad that this compromise did not come from God. So there is found in the Qur'an a clear refusal of such a compromise.

Are you to have the male and He the female? That would be a most unjust distribution—These are nothing but names you have invented yourselves, you and your forefathers. God has sent no authority for them. These people merely follow guesswork and the whims of their souls, even though guidance has come to them from their Lord.   *wa-la-qad jâ'a-hum min rabbi-him al-hudâ*
   (Q 53:21-23)

Let us return to *sûrat al-ḥajj*, "The Pilgrimage," (Q 22) in which reassurance is given for the fight against the wiles of Satan:

> But God removes what Satan insinuates and then God affirms His message. God is all knowing and wise: He makes Satan's insinuations a temptation (*fitna*) only for the sick at heart and those whose hearts are hardened—the evildoers are profoundly opposed [to the Truth]—and He causes those given knowledge to realize that this Revelation is your Lord's Truth, so that they may believe in it and humble their hearts to Him:

God guides the faithful to the straight path. (Q 22:52-54)	*wa-inna Llâha la-hâdî lladhîna âmanû ilâ ṣirâṭ*ⁱⁿ *mustaqîm*

It should cause no surprise that temptations arise and that they can take the form of compromises that could apparently work in our favor. Conscious of this state of affairs, we must always pray for divine guidance:

Guide us on the straight path. (Q 1:6)	*ihdi-nâ l-ṣirâta l-mustaqîm*

Abdel Haleem's translation has been slightly modified here, for it should be noticed that the verb *guide* takes a direct object. We are not asking to be directed *to* the straight path—and once we have reached it we will be able to manage for ourselves (that would be semi-Pelagianism)—but to be guided *on* or *along* the straight path. In other words, there is, and there needs to be, a continual dependence on God; we are to remain constantly under His guidance. It has even been suggested that this guidance *(hudâ)* is the Islamic correspondence to the Christian belief in the Holy Spirit that God gives us as our guide.

In conjunction with this idea of guidance we find another Name of God, *al-nûr*, Light.[4] This is one of the few Names, together with *al-salâm*, Peace, *al-ḥaqq*, Truth or Reality, and *al-ᶜadl*, Justice or Just, which is not based on a verb of action. There is a well-known passage in the Qur'an in which this Name appears, in the *sûra* of the same name, *al-nûr*, Light:

> God is the light of the heavens
>   and earth.   *Allâhu nûr al-samawâti wa-l-ᶜarḍ*
> His Light is like this: there is a niche, and in it a lamp,
> the lamp inside a glass, a glass like a glittering star,
> fuelled from a blessed olive tree from neither east nor west,
> whose oil almost gives light even when no fire touches it—
> light upon light—God guides whoever He will to His light.
>   (Q 24:35)   *yahdî Llâhu li-nûri-hi man yashâ'u*

This is not the place to give a complete exegesis of this passage, but it seems appropriate to underline three characteristics of this light, which represents God:

- It is constant: the lamp is always in the niche;
- It is universal: the olive tree that provides the oil for the lamp is neither from the East nor the West:
- It is pure: the glass is like a sparkling star, and the oil would give light without even being lit.

---

[4] On this Name, in addition to the reference given by Gimaret in n. 1, see al-Ghazâlî, *The Ninety-Nine Beautiful Names*, p.145; see also EI², s.v. "Nur," and EQ, s.v. "Light," p. 187.

It is good to note also the connection with the direction given by God. This is only normal, because darkness is associated with being lost.

Finally, attention can be called to the continuation of the passage. The light is

> shining out in houses of worship. God knew that they would be raised high and His name be remembered in them, with men in them celebrating His glory morning and evening: men who are not distracted, either by commerce or profit, from remembering God, keeping up the prayer, and paying the prescribed alms.
> (Q 24:36-37)

These verses are understood as referring to monasteries in the desert. Their lights would be seen from far away, and travelers could direct their path toward them, knowing that they would find hospitality. They would also find there men dedicated to the praise of God. This underlines the importance of prayer and of disinterested charity as forming part of witness if it is to be effective.

Bound up with the movement from darkness to light, we find another Name of God (*al-walî*),[5] the Protector or the Reigning, translated in the following passage as Ally:

> God is the ally
>   of those who believe: *Allâhu waliyyu lladhîna âmanû*
> He brings them out of the depths of darkness and into the light.
>   (Q 2:257)

---

[5] Cf. al-Ghazâlî, *The Ninety-Nine Beautiful Names*, p. 127; on p. 140 al-Ghazâlî presents the Name *al-wâlî*, "the Ruler." Gimaret discusses these Names in chapter 16, "Souverain"; cf. *Les noms divins*, pp. 313–26, in particular pp. 323–26; see also EI², s.v. "Wali."

The root WLY means "to be near." So in some countries *al-wâlî* is the title given to a Governor who administers a governorate (*wilâya*). There are, therefore, other translations for this Name besides those already mentioned: friend, patron, defender. The term is also used for a saint (*walî,* plural *awliyâ'*), since the saint is close to God and is indeed God's friend, one who has acquired to a notable extent the good qualities of God.

In using this Name for God, the Qur'an emphasizes the mystery of the divine will and also the Oneness of God:

> If God had so pleased, He could have made them a single community, but He admits to His mercy whoever He will; the evildoers will have no one to protect or help them.
>
> *mâ la-hum min waliyyin wa-lâ naṣîrin*
>
> How can they take protectors other than Him?
> God alone is the Protector.   *fa-Llâhu huwa l-walî*
>   (Q 42:8-9)

We can say that it is in God alone, the sole Master, Protector, and Guide, that we are to place our trust.

2. *The OT*

The clearest example of the God who guides is found in the Book of Exodus. The Lord leads His people from the land of bondage to the Promised Land.

> The Lord went in front of them in a pillar of cloud by day, to lead them along the way, and in a pillar of fire by night. Neither the pillar of cloud by day nor the pillar of fire by night left its place in front of the people. (Exod 13:21-22)

We may notice in the first place that there is no rest with regard to following the Lord, or, to put it another way, our rest is to be regulated according to our decision to follow the Lord.

Second, we see that the Lord manifests Himself in different ways. He is not always present in the same manner. It is up to us to discern His presence and to welcome it.

The account of this long march with the Lord continues:

> The angel of God who was going before the Israelite army moved and went behind them; and the pillar of cloud moved from in front of them and took its place behind them. It came between the army of Egypt and the army of Israel. And so the cloud was there with the darkness, and it lit up the night; one did not come near the other all night. (Exod 14:19-20)

This is another way of guiding, by taking up the defense, by becoming the Protector. We may remember the Names of God associated with that of the Rock:

> I love you, O LORD, my strength.
> The Lord is my rock, my fortress, and my deliverer,
>   my God, my rock in whom I take refuge,
>   my shield, and the horn of my salvation, my stronghold.
>   (Ps 18 [17]:1-2)

We have here a veritable cascade of Names of God. We can also say that the very presence of the Lord is already a promise of protection.

The Lord continues to lead the people toward the Promised Land. It is interesting to see the account that the Book of Numbers gives of this progress:

> On the day the tabernacle was set up, the cloud covered the tab-
> ernacle, the tent of the covenant; and from evening until morning
> it was over the tabernacle, having the appearance of fire. It was
> always so: the cloud covered it by day and the appearance of fire by
> night. Whenever the cloud lifted from over the tent, then the Isra-
> elites would set out; and in the place where the cloud settled down,
> there the Israelites would camp. At the command of the LORD the
> Israelites would set out, and at the command of the LORD they
> would camp. As long as the cloud would rest over the tabernacle,
> they would remain in camp. . . . According to the command
> of the LORD they would remain in camp; then according to the
> command of the LORD they would set out. (Num 9:15-18, 20)

In the *Traduction Oecuménique de la Bible* it is explained that a
distinction is to be made between two different things: the tent
was placed outside the camp, whereas the tabernacle was at its
center. In the account given in Numbers the two are rolled into
one. The cloud, which covers the tent/tabernacle day and night,
becomes luminous at night, providing in this way a sign for the
people. The people of Israel are not able to do as they wish. They
are to obey God after reading the signs He gives. Their conduct
must be based on a constant practice of discernment.

The people, however, are not obedient; they are stiff-necked.
They show themselves to be unfaithful, because they make for
themselves a calf to represent their gods. So the Lord says to Moses:

> Go, leave this place, you and the people whom you have brought
> up out of the land of Egypt, and go to the land of which I swore
> to Abraham, Isaac, and Jacob, saying "To your descendants I will
> give it." I will send an angel before you . . . but I will not go up
> among you, or I would consume you on the way, for you are a
> stiff-necked people. (Exod 33:1-3)

These words prove to us that God is not a machine, but truly a person. Are we ready to accept God's freedom? Do we accept that, because of our sins, God does not always manifest Himself to us? The people, having heard the harsh words that God had spoken to Moses, took to mourning. Are we able to draw lessons from the "desolation" (in the Ignatian sense of the word) that we experience, whether we meet this desolation in our prayer or in our everyday life? Are we really ready to let ourselves be led by God?

The Shepherd

When we speak of God as guide we think spontaneously, and with good reason, of the Shepherd.[6]

The LORD is my shepherd. (Ps 23[22]:1)

Psalm 23 (22) is a hymn of trust. The Lord provides nourishment by leading to good pastures; He gives life, for He "restores my soul." Even in the midst of difficulties, "the darkest valley," He is present, and He shows his skill as a shepherd, for "He leads me in right paths."

In Ps 80 [79] this guidance passes from the personal to the collective level:

Give ear, O Shepherd of Israel. (Ps 80 [79]:1)

This psalm gives the impression that it is by means of his bounty, his favor, that the Lord leads. This is indicated by the refrain:

---

[6] Cf. ABD, s.vv. "Sheep," "Shepherd," in particular 5:1189 on God as Shepherd in the OT.

Restore us, O God;
let your face shine, that we may be saved. (Ps 80 [79]:3, 7, 19)

To be looked upon by a benevolent God, to experience the harmony of a peaceful relationship with God, to taste the peace of such a relationship, this is the criterion for discerning how we are to behave. Is not this the real meaning of the instruction given by the prophet Jeremiah?

Thus says the LORD:
Stand at the crossroads, and look,
and ask for the ancient paths,
where the good way lies; and walk in it,
and find rest for your souls. (Jer 6:16)

It is, above all, the prophet Ezekiel who develops the image of God as Shepherd. Unhappy with the shepherds of Israel who are only looking after themselves, God declares:

I myself will search for my sheep, and will seek them out.
(Ezek 34:11)

God has pity on the sheep who are scattered for lack of a good shepherd, and He is going to bring them back into one fold. He will ensure that they are led to good pastures, and He will take particular care of the weak. Yet this good shepherd is also a judge:

I shall judge between sheep and sheep, between rams and goats.
(Ezek 34:17)

Against the bullying tendencies of the strong, He will uphold the weak. But He is also going to make sure of their future:

> I will set up over them one shepherd, my servant David, and he shall feed them: he shall feed them and be their shepherd. And I, the LORD, will be their God, and my servant David shall be prince among them. (Ezek 34:23-24)

God will establish a covenant with this flock, a covenant that leads to communion:

> I will make with them a covenant of peace and banish wild animals from the land, so that they may live in the wild and sleep in the woods securely. . . . You are my sheep, the sheep of my pasture, and I am your God, says the Lord GOD. (Ezek 34:25, 31)

God Light

> The Lord is my light and my salvation. (Ps 27 [26]:1)

This would seem to be the only text in the OT in which Light would appear to be a Name of God. The theme of light is frequent, however, often connected with that of the face of the Lord.

> Let the light of your face shine on us, O LORD. (Ps 4:6)

> Happy are the people who know the festal shout,
>   who walk, O LORD, in the light of your countenance.
>   (Ps 89 [88]:15)

> May God be gracious to us and bless us
>   and make his face to shine upon us. (Ps 67 [66]:1)

This light on the face of God is also an instrument of justice:

> You have set our iniquities before you,
>   our secret sins in the light of your countenance. (Ps 90 [89]:8)

For the LORD is righteous;
he loves righteous deeds;
the upright shall behold his face. (Ps 11 [10]:7)

Or, according to another reading of this last line, one that changes the perspective: "His face looks on righteousness." It is as if God cannot bear evil, and does not even wish to see it.

At the same time, He looks upon the poor with compassion:

For he did not despise or abhor
the affliction of the afflicted;
he did not hide his face from me,
but heard when I cried to him. (Ps 22 [21]:24)

The face of God, when it shines, becomes a source of salvation:

Restore us, O LORD God of hosts;
let your face shine, that we may be saved. (Ps 80 [79]:19)

To be in the presence of the Lord—sometimes translated as being before His face—is also a cause of joy. This is true of the king, of whom it is said:

You bestow on him blessings forever;
you make him glad with the joy of your presence. (Ps 21[20]:6)

But it is also true of the ordinary believer:

You show me the path of life.
In your presence there is the fullness of joy. (Ps 16 [15]:11).

We have come back to the Lord who guides, who makes known the path to follow. Yet, this teaching of the Psalms would seem to find a reflection in the encyclical letter *Spe Salvi* of Pope

Benedict XVI. In speaking of judgment as "a time of apprentice-ship, an experience of hope," Pope Benedict says:

> The encounter with him is the decisive act of judgment. Before his gaze all falsehood melts away. This encounter with him, as it burns us, transforms and frees us, allowing us to become truly ourselves. . . . His gaze, the touch of his heart heals us through an undeniably painful transformation "as through fire." But it is a blessed pain, in which the holy power of his love sears through us like a flame, enabling us to become totally ourselves and thus totally of God.[7]

Have we strayed from our topic, the God who guides? We have, at any rate, arrived already at the perspective given by the NT.

3. *The NT*

The Shepherd

Through the words of the prophet Ezekiel, God has presented Himself as the shepherd of His people. According to the Gospel of John, in chapter 10, Jesus applies this title to himself. Before this, however, he identifies himself with the gate of the sheepfold:

Very truly, I tell you, I am the gate for the sheep. (John 10:7)

So Jesus gives himself a new Name, and through a very solemn proclamation. The use in this context of the divine Name found in Exodus, "I am," emphasizes the divinity of Jesus. This recourse

---

[7] Benedict XVI, *Spe Salvi*, no.47, at http://w2.vatican.va/content/benedict -xvi/en/encyclicals/documents/hf_ben-xvi_enc_20071130_spe-salvi.html.

to "I am" is frequent in the Gospel of John.[8] Here Jesus proclaims that he is the way that one must follow in order to enter into life. It is through the gate that the true shepherd enters, and this shepherd knows his sheep, and they know him and recognize his voice. There is, we could say, communion in mutual knowledge, just as Jesus will present as model the communion that exists between himself and the Father, a communion in the Spirit (cf. John 10:14-15).

The shepherd walks ahead of his sheep; he acts as their guide. Moreover, Jesus, the Good Shepherd, is ready to sacrifice his life for the sheep: "I lay down my life for the sheep" (John 10:15). For this reason, the Father loves him. The Father has given all things to the Son (cf. John 16:15), and Jesus, following this example, gives all things. Like Father, like Son! Is this reasonable, or does it seem unreasonable? Are we ready to accept the law of the Gospel: "For those who want to save their life will lose it, and those who lose their life for my sake will find it" (Matt 16: 25)?

Jesus, the Shepherd, is also the Lamb. Through his incarnation the Son of God has become identified with the sheep of his flock. According to the vision portrayed in the book of Revelation, the Lamb has conquered death, because the Lamb is "standing," although it is as if it has been "slaughtered." The Lamb is the victim that has been offered once and for all, but that in fact is offered for the whole of eternity (cf. Rev 5:6). By dying it has conquered death and has entered into life, becoming itself the source of life. In this image of the Lamb, slaughtered but standing, the whole paschal mystery is presented.

---

[8] Cf. JB on John 6:20, p. 159, n. *i*; see also the TOB on the same passage, p. 306, n. *r*.

The book of Revelation also describes the heavenly liturgy that surrounds the Lamb (cf. Rev 5:7-14). We are invited to associate ourselves with this liturgy of adoration and to unite our praises with those that are offered by the heavenly court. For this we must put on the nuptial garment; in other words, we must allow ourselves to be purified by the blood of the Lamb.

A curious thing is that this Lamb that has been slaughtered, and that is worthy to receive "power and wealth and wisdom and might and honor and glory and blessing" (Rev 5:12), is at the same time the Shepherd who guides to the springs of the water of life (cf. Rev 7:17). It is necessary to follow the Lamb "wherever he goes" (Rev 14:4) and finally to the marriage supper of the Lamb: "Blessed are those who are invited to the marriage supper of the Lamb" (Rev 19:9).

God Light

In the heavenly city of which the book of Revelation gives us a glimpse, where there is no longer any Temple, and where the throne is in the middle of the city (not like the cross, the throne of the suffering Christ that was located outside the city), there will be no further need of the sun or of the moon as sources of light, "for the glory of God is its light, and its lamp is the Lamb" (Rev 21:23).

The prophet Isaiah had already identified the Servant (whether representing the whole people of God or an individual chosen by God) with the light. The Lord, who had called this servant from the time he was in his mother's womb, said to him:

> It is too light a thing that you should be my servant
> > to raise up the tribes of Jacob
> > and to restore the survivors of Israel;

> I will give you as a light to the nations,
>> that my salvation shall reach to the end of the earth. (Isa 49:6)

Following this Servant, Jerusalem must be transformed into light in order to bear witness and to radiate, thus attracting the nations.

The NT sees in this Servant a figure of Jesus. Jesus declared himself to be light:

> I am the light of the world. Whoever follows me will never walk in darkness but will have the light of life. (John 8:12)

After having given sight to a man born blind, Jesus declared:

> As long as I am in the world, I am the light of the world. (John 9:5)

He is, in fact, the Word that the prologue of John's Gospel identifies with the light:

> The true light, which enlightens everyone, was coming into the world. (John 1:9)

He does not leave those who believe in him in the darkness (cf. John 12:46). To come out of the darkness, however, one must believe and also act in conformity with this faith. We shall be judged according to the way we react to the light:

> And this is the judgment, that the light has come into the world, and people loved darkness rather than light because their deeds were evil. For all who do evil hate the light and do not come to the light, so that their deeds may not be exposed. But those who do what is true come to the light, so that it may be clearly seen that their deeds have been done in God. (John 3:19-21)

We can examine our consciences. Do we really want to seek the truth and walk in the light, or are we content to remain in darkness? Even if this darkness is not total, embracing the whole of our life, but restricted to some areas of it, this can prevent us from moving forward. Jesus has said:

> We must work the works of him who sent me while it is day; night is coming when no one can work. As long as I am in the world, I am the light of the world.[9] (John 9:4-5)

If I am not able to follow Christ the Light as I should and as I wish to do, if I remain partly in blindness, then I should seek out someone to help me. It is not easy to accept to subject oneself to the opinion of another, or to that of the community; this requires a high degree of humility. The experience of the Church, however, teaches us that such help is most useful and indeed almost necessary. What is important above all is that we faithfully follow Jesus.

[9] The NRSV notes a variant: "I must work" The choice of the plural "we" is justified by the *Traduction Oecuménique de la Bible*, which points out that the well-attested plural would seem to indicate that the Christian community considered its own action as a continuation of that of Christ; cf. TOB on John 9:4, p. 317 n. *x*. On all these texts of the Gospel of John see Francis J. Moloney, *The Gospel of John*: on the prologue, pp. 34–41 ; on 3:19, p. 96 ; on 8:12, pp. 266, 268; on 9:4-5, pp. 291–92, 297.

VII

The God Who Is Generous and Faithful

The God who guides us is not ungenerous; He is not stingy. He does not want to give us only "sufficient grace." He wants to shower his gifts on us, as He did upon Mary "the highly favored one." The All-mighty God is mighty in goodness. So we are invited to what St. Ignatius of Loyola calls the *contemplatio ad amorem,* a contemplation of the love that flows from the Lord. To that is added a reflection on the Faithful God, a God on whom we can really count.

1. *The Teaching of the Qur'an*

Proclaim![1]	
Your Lord is	
the Most Bountiful One.	*iqra' wa-rabbu-ka l-akram*
(Q 96:3-5)	

[1] Here the reading of Yusuf Ali is preferred to that of Abdel Haleem, who translates "Read!"

In this passage of the Qur'an, recognized by all to be the first chronologically, the generosity of God is proclaimed. The root of the term used, KRM, has a twofold meaning: it indicates both nobility and generosity. In fact the two are linked, since generosity is a proof of nobility.[2] In pre-Islamic Arab society liberality, even to excess, was a characteristic of the great leader. This is still true of Arab society, whether Christian or Muslim, where the guest will be honored with an abundance of dishes.

In the Qur'an the adjective *karîm*[3] is used more often of things than of people. We hear of a noble letter, *kitâb karîm* (Q 27:29), of a respectful word or speech "in terms of honor," *qawl karîm* (Q 17:23), of a shadow of black smoke in Hell that is "neither cool, nor refreshing," *lâ bârid wa-lâ karîm* (Q 56:44)—perhaps in this case "welcoming" would be a more apt rendering. In speaking of creation, the Qur'an mentions a "noble pair," *zawj karîm,* translated as "noble kinds of thing" (Q 26:7; 31:10). The Qur'an speaks of a noble reward, *ajr karîm*, which one assumes would be generous (Q 36:11; 57:11.17), as also of a generous provision, *rizq karîm* (Q 8:4; 8:74; 22:50; 24:29; 34:4), for the true believers who live according to their faith. We find "an entrance of honour," *madkhal karîm*, as a description of the entrance to Paradise (Q 4:31). The adjective is used just once for the Qur'an itself, *qur'ân karîm* (56:77), but this will become the customary way of talking about it, *al-qur'ân al-karîm*, the Noble Qur'an.

[2] Cf. EI[2] Supplement, s.v. "Karam."

[3] On *al-karîm* as a Name for God see al-Ghazâlî, *The Ninety-Nine Beautiful Names*, pp. 113–14. Gimaret discusses the Name *al-karîm*, as well as that of *al-akram*, in his chapter titled "Parfait," *Les noms divins*, pp. 219–22.

Karîm is also used to qualify persons. In the story of Joseph, the women invited by the governor's wife exclaim on seeing Joseph: "Great God! He cannot be mortal! He must be 'a precious angel,'" *malak karîm* (Q 12:31). The expression "a noble messenger," *rasûl karîm*, is used for Moses (Q 44:17) as also of Muhammad (Q 69:40; 81:19).

It is worth considering the following passage:

> Exalted be God, the true King, there is no god but Him,
> the Lord of the Glorious Throne.   *rabb al-ʿarsh al-karîm*
>   (Q 23:116)

It would seem that the nobility has been passed from the person to the thing, the throne.[4] God is indeed called generous, *rabbuka l-karîm* (Q 82:6), and *Allâh karîm* comes frequently to the tongues of Arabs who trust that God will make all things turn out right. If God is the best of Creators, it can be said that He is also the Most Generous among the generous: he is *al-akram*.

The Name *karîm*, noble, generous, occurs at the end of the story of Solomon in *sûrat al-niml*, the Ants (Q 27). It may be useful to consider the whole passage.

> And we gave knowledge to David and Solomon, and they both
> said, "Praise be to God, who has favored us over many of his
> believing servants." (Q 27:15)

There is here a loving preference that is noteworthy. It will be present also in the case of Mary.

---

[4] Gimaret notes, however, that the commentator of the Qur'an, Zamakhsharî, followed by Râzî and by Baydâwî, records the reading *huwa rabbu l-ʿarshi l-karîmu*, "the Lord of the Throne, the Generous One," cf. *Les noms divins*, p. 220.

The angels said to Mary, "Mary, God has chosen you and made
you pure: He has truly chosen you above all women." (Q 3:42)

Solomon recognizes the great favor that God has shown him:

We have been given a share of everything: this is clearly a great
favor. (Q 27:16)

The realization of having received so much—and this includes
the ability to understand the language of creatures, including the
ant—arouses in Solomon a great sense of gratitude:

Lord, inspire me to be thankful for the blessings You have granted
me and my parents, and to do good deeds that please You; admit
me by Your grace into the ranks of Your righteous servants.
(Q 27:19)

The hoopoe informs Solomon of the beauty of the Queen of Sheba,
Bilqis (the name is not found in the Qur'an, but comes from tradition),[5] who also has been given a share of everything. Yet, Bilqis
and her people adore the sun instead of the true God. So Solomon
sends her "a gracious letter," *kitâb^{un} karîm*, which reads:

In the name of God, the Lord of Mercy, the Giver of Mercy,
do not put yourselves above me,
and come to me in submission to God.   *muslimîn*
(Q 27:30-31)

The Queen of Sheba sends rich gifts to Solomon, gifts that he
does not need and that make him suspicious:

<hr />

[5] Cf. EI², s.v. "Bilḳis," as also EQ, s.v. "*Bilqis*."

What God has given me is better than what He has given you. (Q 27:36)

He decides to march against this people, but beforehand he asks if anyone is capable of bringing to him the Queen's great throne. This is achieved, and when the throne is set before him he cries out:

This is a favor from my Lord	*hâḏa min faḏli rabbî*
to test whether I am grateful or not.	*li-yablua-nî a-ash-*
	kuru am akfuru

Solomon recognizes that he could become swollen with pride and could forget God: he could become a *kâfir*, someone who is ungrateful or an unbeliever. The Qur'anic text continues:

If anyone is grateful, it is for his own good,	
if anyone is ungrateful,	
then my Lord is self-sufficient	
and most generous.	*fa-inna rabbî ghaniyy^{un} karîm*
(Q 27:40)	

In other words, *kufr*, ingratitude or unbelief, has no effect on God, but because He is *karîm,* He will give His grace so that the one who is destined to believe may have faith.

We see, then, that this fine story ends with the Queen of Sheba making a confession of faith:

My Lord, I have wronged myself: I devote myself, with Solomon, to God, the Lord of the worlds. (Q 27:44)

Frequently in the Qur'an the remark is made that the goodness of God is often not acknowledged:

God shows real favor to people, but most of them are ungrateful.
(Q 2:243)

Nevertheless God, as we have seen, is generous:

Who will give God a good loan, which He will increase for him many times over?	
It is God who withholds	
and God who gives abundantly.	*wa-Llâhu yaqbiḍ wa-yabsiṭ*
(Q 2:245)	

This verse provides us with two more Names of God: *al-qâbiḍ*, He who restrains, and *al-bâsiṭ*, He who expands.[6]

Even as the Lord guides us, we must continue to ask him to fill us with his gifts. We can do this with confidence since He is *al-wahhâb*, The Constant Giver.[7]

Our Lord, do not let our hearts deviate after you have guided us.	
Grant us Your mercy:	*wahab la-nâ min ladun-ka raḥmat^{an}*
You are the Ever Giving.	*inna-ka anta l-wahhâb*
(Q 3:8; cf. 38:9, 35)	

---

[6] Cf. al-Ghazâlî, *The Ninety-Nine Beautiful Names*, pp. 81–82. These two Names are examined together by Gimaret in the chapter "Maître des destinées," "Master of destiny," *Les noms divins*, pp. 333–35. God gives sustenance (*rizq*), to some abundantly, to others sparingly. Some authors give a different interpretation of these Names: God is *bâsiṭ* in so far as he has "extended" the earth at the time of creation; on the Day of Resurrection He will be *qâbiḍ* when He will gather all things in His hand. The Sufis understand these Names in relation to the hearts of the believers: God, *al-qâbiḍ*, makes these hearts contract by inspiring them with fear, and as *al-bâsiṭ* He dilates them by filling them with hope.

[7] Cf. al-Ghazâlî, *The Ninety-Nine Beautiful Names*, pp. 74–78; Gimaret, *Les noms divins*, pp. 400–401.

We are always in need of God's help; we can never do without Him. He alone is *al-ghanî*, the All-Sufficient. We have always to receive our daily bread, whether material or spiritual, *al-rizq*, from the one who is *al-razzâq,* the Provider.[8]

If God is the Constant Giver, there must be constancy also on the side of the one who is receiving divine gifts. If God is *al-ṣabûr*, the Very Patient (a Name that does not appear as such in the Qur'an),[9] then human beings also must show endurance. The final reward is for

> Those who fulfil the agreements they make in God's name and
> do not break their pledges. . . .

Who remain steadfast	*alladîna ṣabarû*
through their desire for the face	
of their Lord.	*ibtighâ'an wajha rabbi-him*

to whom it will be said:

Peace be with you,	*salâm ʿalay-kum*
Because you have remained steadfast.	*bi-mâ ṣabartum*
(Q 13:20-24)	

2. *The OT*

"Fidelity (Heb. *emet*) is a major attribute of God (cf. Exod 34:6), and is often associated with paternal goodness (Heb. *hesed*)

---

[8] On the meaning of *rizq* and of the two Names *al-râziq* and *al-razzâq* see Gimaret, *Les noms divins*, pp. 397–400; see al-Ghazâlî, *The Ninety-Nine Beautiful Names*, pp. 78–79; see also EQ, s.v. "Sustenance."

[9] On this Name, see al-Ghazâlî, *The Ninety-Nine Beautiful Names*, pp. 148–49, as also Gimaret, *Les noms divins*, p. 422, who classes it with *al-ghafûr* and *al-ghaffâr* among the Names that express divine forbearance. God is never precipitate. He is ever "the One who does not hasten to punish."

toward the people of the covenant. These two complementary attributes are an indication that the covenant is at one and the same time a free gift from God and a binding link, the solidity of which has been proved down the centuries (cf. Ps 119:90)."[10]

The meaning of *hesed* is that God is committed to the people with whom He has established a covenantal relationship. While remaining completely free and in no way subject to pressure, He provides for all their needs. The following are the key elements of this goodness: to maintain creation, to allow the people to continue through their descendants, to give the necessary sustenance for each day, to give protection, to raise up leaders to guide the people, to be always ready to grant pardon.[11]

To come to an understanding of this paternal goodness it would be sufficient to read the chapters in the book of Exodus that relate how God took care of His people, guiding them and nourishing them (Exod 16–17). This aspect of God's care is taken up in the Psalms, where divine *hesed* is mentioned more than seventy times. Here is an example:

> These all look to you
>> to give them their food in due season;
> when you give it to them, they gather it up;
>> when you open your hand, they are filled with good things.
>> (Ps 104 [103]:27-28)

The Psalms also sing of God's fidelity:

> Praise the LORD, all you nations!
>> Extol him, all you peoples!

---

[10] Xavier Léon-Dufour, *Vocabulaire de théologie biblique*, s.v. "Fidélité."
[11] Cf. ABD, s.v. "Love."

> For great is his steadfast love toward us,
>> and the faithfulness of the LORD endures forever.
>>> (Ps 117 [116]:1-2)

> For the LORD is good;
>> his steadfast love endures forever,
> and his faithfulness to all generations. (Ps 100 [99]:5)

The Lord is always true to His word. This is why we can always count on Him. The diviner Balaam[12] states this quite roundly:

> God is not a human being, that he should lie,
>> or a mortal, that he should change his mind.
> He has promised, and will he not do it?
>> He has spoken, and will he not fulfill it? (Num 23:19)

The contrast between the human and the divine is stark:

> All people are grass,
>> their constancy is like the flower of the field.
> The grass withers, the flower fades,
>> when the breath of the LORD blows upon it;
>>> surely the people are grass.
> The grass withers, the flower fades;
>> but the word of our God will stand forever. (Isa 40:6-8)

Elsewhere the prophet Isaiah extols God for his faithfulness:

> O LORD, you are my God;
>> I will exalt you, I will praise your name;
> for you have done wonderful things,
>> plans formed of old, faithful and sure. (Isa 25:1)

---

[12] On this strange figure, see the note in the *Traduction Oecuménique de la Bible* on Num 22:2, p. 304, n. *k*.

3. *The NT*

The Gospels present us with the image of the God who is Most Generous, and we are invited to follow the example given:

> Be merciful, just as your Father is merciful. . . . Give and it will be given to you. A good measure, pressed down, shaken together, running over, will be put into your lap. For the measure you give will be the measure you get back. (Luke 6:36-38)

Jesus encourages his disciples to have confidence in divine bounty:

> Consider the ravens: they neither sow nor reap, they have neither storehouse nor barn, and yet God feeds them. Of how much more value are you than the birds! . . . Consider the lilies, how they grow: they neither toil nor spin; yet I tell you, even Solomon in all his glory was not clothed like one of these. . . . Strive for his kingdom, and these things will be given to you as well.
>
> Do not be afraid, little flock, for it is your Father's good pleasure to give you the kingdom. (Luke 12:24, 27, 31-32)

Jesus acts in the same way as the Father. When he nourishes the crowd, he does not give them just a bare sufficiency; what remains over after all have satisfied their hunger is enough to fill twelve baskets (cf. Luke 9:10-17). Yet the supreme proof of his love, love of an excessive kind, we might be tempted to say, is the very gift of his own life:

> Now before the festival of the Passover, Jesus knew that his hour had come to depart from this world and go to the Father. Having loved his own who were in the world, he loved them to the end. (John 13:1)

The Apostle John meditates on this gift of love that reflects the love of the Father and serves as an example for us:

> Beloved, let us love one another, because love is from God; everyone who loves is born of God and knows God. Whoever does not love does not know God, for God is love. (1 John 4:7-8)

Here is revealed the true Name of God; we would be tempted to say God's "Supreme Name." The text continues:

> God's love was revealed among us in this way: God sent his only Son into the world so that we might live through him. In this is love, not that we loved God but that he loved us and sent his Son to be the atoning sacrifice for our sins. (1 John 4:9-10)

The apostle Paul presents Jesus as an example. He writes to the Corinthians:

> For you know the generous act of our Lord Jesus Christ, that though he was rich, yet for our sakes he became poor, so that by his poverty you may become rich. (2 Cor 8:9)

The love of God, made manifest in the gift of the Son, is characterized by fidelity. Paul underlines this when reflecting on the mystery of Israel:

> As regards the gospel they are enemies of God for your sake; but as regards election they are beloved, for the gifts and the calling of God are irrevocable. (Rom 11:28-29)

This reflection is extremely important. We must be careful not to adopt the idea of abrogation. The covenant with the people of Israel continues, even if it has been renewed; this covenant is not abrogated but persists, as Jesus himself has said:

> Do not think that I have come to abolish the law or the prophets; I have not come to abolish but to fulfill.(Matt 5:17)

God is faithful to his chosen people, but he is at the same time faithful to each one of us. Paul reassures us:

> God is faithful, and he will not let you be tested beyond your strength, but with the testing he will also provide the way out so that you may be able to endure it. (1 Cor 10:13)

At the beginning of this First Letter to the Corinthians, Paul meditates on the goodness and the fidelity of the Lord. He gives thanks:

> I give thanks to my God always for you because of the grace of God that has been given you in Christ Jesus, for in every way you have been enriched in him, in speech and knowledge of every kind. . . .
>
> He will also strengthen you to the end, so that you may be blameless on the day of our Lord Jesus Christ. God is faithful; by him you were called into the fellowship of his Son, Jesus Christ our Lord. (1 Cor 1:4-9)

We can therefore make our own the prayer of Paul in which he asks that the Christians of Ephesus be "filled with all the fullness of God":

> Now to him who by the power at work within us is able to accomplish abundantly far more than all we can ask or imagine, to him be glory in the church and in Christ Jesus to all generations, forever and ever. Amen. (Eph 3:20-21)

What happened in the case of Mary can serve as a coda to this meditation. The angel announces to her that she is the "favored one," favored by God, it is understood. How does Mary react? She is "much perplexed" by these words (Luke 1:28-29).[13] What

---

[13] In a note in the *Traduction Oecuménique de la Bible* it is observed that the verb used here is much stronger than the one used in the case of Zechariah in

does this greeting mean? We see a constant here with regard to the mystery of love, whether it be divine love or human love. The question always arises: how is it that I am loved, by another human being, by Jesus, by God the Father? Am I really lovable? The angel explains to Mary: you have found favor with God. Is it because she is pure, because she is truly beautiful, literally graceful, that she has found favor with God to the point of being chosen as the mother of His Son? We believe not that Mary has been chosen because of her purity or her beauty, but rather that she is all pure, immaculate, on account of her election by God for this special role. Can one explain the love that is felt for a person on the basis of the beauty or the qualities of that person? Is it not true that love often creates, or helps to create, the qualities and the true beauty of the beloved? For love gives confidence; love is a liberating force, the source of new transforming energy. So Mary replies:

> Here am I, the servant of the Lord; let it be with me according to your word. (Luke 1:38)

Luke 1:12, for the angel's greeting to Mary suggests that she has a quite singular vocation; see TOB, p. 192, n. *c*.

VIII

God, Our Peace

How should these reflections on the Beautiful Names of God be concluded? One way is to meditate on God who constitutes Himself our reward, God, our Peace, God the First and the Last, God, the Eternal and Everlasting One. This will be an anticipation of our final destiny at which we are invited to enter into the fullness of God. It is a meditation that can sustain us while we are still *in via,* on the way.

1. *The Teaching of the Qur'an*

> He is God: there is no other god but him,
> The King, the Holy One,
> Source of Peace.   *al-salâm*
>   (Q 59:23)

We have already considered this text when discussing the Names "King" and "Holy One." Now our focus is the Name "Peace," which occurs only in this text.

How is this Name to be understood? The Arabic word *salâm* means, in the first place, soundness, being unimpaired, intactness, and so well-being; it also means safety, security, and finally peace. As can be seen from the translation of the Qur'anic passage given above, for Abdel Haleem it would appear insufficient to call God simply Peace. He feels the need to indicate that God is the source of peace. Gimaret, in the brief study that he makes of this Name, refuses completely the notion of peace.[1] Following the interpretation given by some theologians, he asserts that *al-salâm* is to be understood as meaning *dhû l-salâma*, possessor of soundness or, put negatively, free of all imperfection. Yusuf Ali would seem to combine the two approaches when he renders the Name "Source of Peace (and Perfection)." Gerhard Böwering offers other possible interpretations: "The One who possesses true peace," "the giver of peace at the dawn of creation and on the day of resurrection," and even "the One who pronounces the blessing of peace over creation."[2]

Perhaps we can come at this obliquely, by looking at another expression in which *salâm* occurs.

> [Prophet], this is the path of your Lord, made perfectly straight. We have explained Our revelations to those who take heed. They shall have the Home of Peace—*dâr al-salâm*—with their Lord, and He will take care of them as a reward for their deeds. (Q 6:126-27)

It is obvious that the text is talking of Paradise, the reward for the just. This will be a place of security, where the Lord Himself will be the *walî* of the just, taking care of them, as Abdel Haleem

---

[1] The Name is discussed in the chapter "Parfait," *Les noms divins*, pp. 204–5. Al-Ghazâlî gives as meaning for this Name: "The Flawless, the one whose essence is free from defect, whose attributes escape imperfection," cf. *The Ninety-Nine Beautiful Names*, p. 61.

[2] Cf. EQ, s.v. "God and His Attributes."

puts it, or as their Friend, according to Yusuf Ali. We could say then that the essential feature of this abode of peace will be the Lord Himself.

Who can enter this Paradise? The Qur'an gives a clear answer to this question:

> There will be the best of rewards for those who respond to their Lord. . .
>
> Those who fulfil the agreements they make in God's name and do not break their pledges; who join together what God commands to be joined; who are in awe of their Lord and fear the harshness of the Reckoning; who remain steadfast through their desire for the face of their Lord; who keep up the prayer; who give secretly and openly from what We have provided for them; who repel evil with good. These will have the reward of the [true] home: they will enter perpetual Gardens, along with their righteous ancestors, spouses, and descendants; the angels will go into them from every gate, "Peace be with you, because you have remained steadfast. *al-salâm ᶜalay-kum bi-mâ ṣabartum*
> What an excellent reward is this home of yours!" (Q 13:18, 20-24)

Many are under the impression that Paradise, for Muslims, is just a place of delights, full of shaded arbors, where nourishment is found in abundance, and where the Houris are at the disposition of the blessed. It is true that the Qur'an describes Paradise in such terms but, if one looks at the texts attentively, one can discern something more. For example:

> No frivolity will they hear therein.
> nor any taint of ill,—
> only the saying, "Peace! Peace."[3] (Q 56:25-26)

[3] Translation of Yusuf Ali.

This peaceful atmosphere is in sharp contrast with the hail of mutual accusations in Hell:

> Every crowd curses its fellow crowd as it enters, then, when they are all gathered inside, the last of them will say of the first, "Our Lord, it was they who led us astray; give them double punishment in the Fire"—God says, "Every one of you will have double punishment, though you do not know it"—and the first of them will say to the last, "You were no better than us; taste the punishment you have earned." (Q 7:38-39)

How different is the situation of the righteous, who enter Paradise purified:

> We shall have removed all ill feeling from their hearts. (Q 7:43)

The term used here, *ghill*, is perhaps stronger than just ill feeling, since it includes spite, malice, rancor, and rank hatred. There is obviously no place for such feelings in Paradise. Those who are judged worthy to enter this abode find themselves greeted with the salutation:

> "Peace be with you."   *salâm^{un} ^{c}alay-kum*
>   (Q 7:46)

This greeting is addressed to each one individually:

> If he is one of those on the Right,
>   [he will hear], "Peace be on you"   *fa-salâm^{un} la-ka*
> from his companions on the Right.
>   (Q 56:91)

Who is responsible for this welcome? We could say that in the final analysis the source of this peace is the Lord of Mercy Himself:

The people of Paradise today[4] are happily occupied—they and
their spouses—seated on couches in the shade. There they have
fruit and whatever they ask for.

"Peace," a word from	
the Lord of Mercy.	*salâm^{un} qawl^{an} min rabb^{in} rahîm*
(Q 36:55-58)	

Everything has its source in God, and all things belong to Him.
From this comes the saying:

"We belong to God,	
and to Him we shall return."	*innâ li-Llâhi wa-ilay-hi râjiʿîn.*

This conviction has an impact on our behavior. It teaches us
that we are not to cling to earthly realities, for everything belongs
to God and lies in His hands.

It is God who will inherit the heavens and earth. | *li-Llâhi mîrâth
al-samawâti wa-l-arḍ*
(Q 3:180)

Why should you not give for God's cause when God alone will
inherit what is in the heavens and earth? (Q 57:10)

From these texts is derived a Name for God that may seem
strange to Christians: *al-wârith,* the Inheritor. It is found in the
Qur'an, plural in form but singular in meaning:

It is We who give life	
and death;	*wa-innâ la-nahnu nuhyî wa-numît*
it is We who inherit	
everything.	*wa-nahnu l-wârithûn*
(Q 15:23)	

---

[4] Or perhaps better "on that Day," *al-yawma*, which is obviously the final
Day of Resurrection.

It is worth noting, in the above verse, the basis for two more Names of God: *al-muḥyî*, the Life-Giver, and *al-mumît*, the Creator of Death.[5]

Zachariah, when praying to God for a son who will be able to inherit from him, recognizes that God is the best of those who inherit:

Remember Zachariah,
when he cried to his Lord,
"My Lord, do not leave me childless,
though you are the best of heirs.   *anta khayru l-wârithîn*
        (Q 21:89)

What does this mean? At the end of the world, on the Day of Resurrection, everything will belong to God. God is, in fact, the Supreme Heir, because in the final analysis only God is Eternal, *al-bâqî*. We find a reference to this fact in the discussion between Pharaoh and his magicians. These magicians, having seen the signs worked by Moses, profess their belief in the God of Moses and Aaron. Pharaoh becomes angry, since they have declared their belief without asking for his permission. He wants to punish them, showing them who is more powerful. Nevertheless the magicians persist in their faith, saying to Pharaoh:

You can only decide matters
    of this present life . . .
God is better, and more lasting.   *wa-Llâhu khayr wa-abqâ*[6]
        (Q 20:72-73)

---

[5] On *al-wârith,* see al-Ghazâlî, *The Ninety-Nine Beautiful Names*, p. 148; and Gimaret, *Les noms divins*, in the chapter "Eternel," p. 186; and on *al-muḥyî* and *al-mumît*, al-Ghazâlî, *The Ninety-Nine Beautiful Names*, pp. 128–29, and Gimaret in the chapter "Maître des destinées," *Les noms divins*, pp. 327–31.

[6] This is the only place in the Qur'an where the term *abqâ* is applied to God.

A passage in *sûrat al-rahmân* gives a clear expression to this truth. After having recalled the marvels of creation, it states:

All that is on earth will perish:	*kullu man ʿalay-hâ fânin*
But will abide [for ever]	
the Face of thy Lord.	*wa-yabqâ wajhu rabbi-ka*
Full of Majesty, Bounty and Honor.	*dhû l-jalâli wa-l-ikrâm*
(Q 55:26-27)[7]	

In this verse we find a Name of God already mentioned in a previous meditation, *dhû l-jalâl wa-l-ikrâm*, the Lord of Majesty and Generosity.[8] From it, too, will be developed the Sufi teaching on *fanâ'*, the disappearance of all that is ephemeral, so that in the end only God remains.[9]

Now if God is all that will remain, will He truly be the Peace of the Blessed? Will the Blessed see God in Paradise? In attempting to answer this question, the following texts can be taken into consideration:

On that Day some faces will be beaming, laughing and rejoicing. (Q 80:38-39)

Some faces on that Day will be radiant with bliss, well pleased with their labor, in a lofty garden, where they will hear no idle talk. (Q 88:8-11)

You will recognize on their faces the radiance of bliss. (Q 83:24)

---

[7] Translation of Yusuf Ali.

[8] Cf. al-Ghazâlî, *The Ninety-Nine Beautiful Names*, p. 140, and Gimaret, *Les noms divins*, pp. 214–15.

[9] Cf. EI², s.v. "*Baḳaʾ wa-fanaʾ*."

They will be served precious wine mixed with water of Tasnim,

> a spring from which those brought near will drink. (Q 83:28)

It seems obvious that those rewarded in this way are those who are brought near to God.

> The righteous will live securely among Gardens and rivers, secure
> in the presence of an all-powerful Sovereign.   *ʿinda malîk^{in}*
>   (Q 54:54-55)[10]   *muqtadar^{in}*

In the state which the blessed will enjoy it is possible to perceive even a certain communion with God:

> [But] you, soul at peace: *yâ-ayyuhâ l-nafsu l-muṭmaʾinna*
> return to your Lord
>   well pleased   *arjiʿî ilâ rabbi-ki râḍiyat^{an}*
> and well pleasing;   *marḍiyya*
> go in among my servants;   *fa-dkhulî fî ʿibâdî*
> and into my Garden.   *wa-dkhulî fî jannatî*
>   (Q 89:27-30)

According to the Qurʾan, therefore, the blessed do not become children of God, but remain His servants; nor do they enter the dwelling of God, but only His garden. Nevertheless, the desire to see God persists:

> But those most devoted to God . . .
> Those who spend their wealth for increase in self-purification,

---

[10] This is the only passage in the Qurʾan in which the form *malîk* is found. It is considered as an intensive form of *malik*, just as *ʿalîm* in relation to *ʿâlim* or *qadîr* in relation to *qâdir*; cf. Gimaret, *Les noms divins*, p. 318.

and have in their minds no favor from anyone
for which a reward is expected in return,
but only the desire to seek for the Countenance of their Lord
    Most High;
and soon will they attain [complete] satisfaction. (Q 92:19-21)[11]

And again:

But Paradise will be brought close to the righteous and will no
    longer be distant:
"This is what you were promised . . .
So enter it in peace. This is the Day of everlasting Life."
They will have all that they wish for there,
and We have more for them.   *wa-laday-nâ mazîd*
    (Q 50:31-32, 34-35)

This something more, will it be to see God? *Allâhu aᶜlam*! God
knows best.

2. *The OT*[12]

"The Hebrew word for peace, *shalom*, expresses far more than
the absence of war; it includes health, fruitfulness, prosperity,
friendship with God and with others."[13] Is it because of this mul-
tiplicity of meanings that the Name "Peace" is rarely used for
God in the Old Testament? In fact there would seem to be only
one single case in which God is identified with peace. This is

[11] Translation according to Yusuf Ali.

[12] Cf. ABD, s.v. "Peace."

[13] Note of the *Traduction Oecuménique de la Bible* on Isaiah 66:12: "For thus
says the Lord: Now towards her I send flowing peace, like a river" (JB); cf. TOB,
p. 881, n. *b*. The NRSV has "prosperity" for peace in this verse.

when Gideon builds an altar to the Lord and calls it: "The Lord
is peace" (Judg 6:24).

God is seen, rather, as the source of peace:

"Great is the LORD,
who likes to see his servant at peace." (Ps 35 [34]:27)[14]

It is God who will establish peace through the promised Messiah:

For a child has been born for us,
a son given to us;
authority rests upon his shoulders;
and he is named
Wonderful Counselor, Mighty God,
Everlasting Father, Prince of Peace.
His authority shall grow continually,
and there shall be endless peace
for the throne of David and his kingdom.
He will establish and uphold it
with justice and with righteousness
from this time onward and for evermore. (Isa 9:6-7)

We may note here the abundance of names given to the Messiah,
names that can be used for Jesus, the Son of David, the Son of God.

In another prophecy concerning the one who is to be born,
this figure is identified with peace:

But you, O Bethlehem of Ephrathah,
who are one of the little clans of Judah,
from you shall come forth for me
one who is to rule in Israel, . . .

[14] Translation of JB. The NRSV has "welfare" instead of peace.

And he shall stand and feed his flock in the strength of the LORD,
    in the majesty of the name of the LORD his God.
And they shall live secure, for now he shall be great
    to the ends of the earth;
    and he shall be the one of peace. (Mic 5:2-5)

Peace thus becomes a sign of the Kingdom of God.

Can we say that the Lord Himself is the reward promised to those who belong to this Kingdom and who strive for its establishment? We do find some references to the idea that God is the inheritance of the just, a lot that has already been given but that will be finally secured in the world to come.

LORD, my heritage, my cup,
    You, and you only, hold my lot secure. (Ps 16 [15]:5 JB)

Whom have I in heaven but you?
      And there is nothing on earth that I desire other than you.
    My flesh and my heart may fail,
but God is the strength of my heart and my portion forever.
(Ps 73 [72]:25-26)

Yes, indeed, God forever, for He is the Eternal One. We find a fine expression of faith in this God in a letter that King Darius writes after Daniel has been delivered from the lions' den:

"May you have abundant prosperity! I make a decree, that in all my royal dominion people should tremble and fear before the God of Daniel:
    For he is the living God,
      enduring forever.
    His kingdom shall never be destroyed,
      and his dominion has no end.

He delivers and rescues,
    he works signs and wonders in heaven and on earth;
for he has saved Daniel
    from the power of the lions." (Dan 6:25-27)

3. *The NT*[15]

The birth of Jesus is the sign and pledge of messianic peace, and so it is quite natural that on the occasion of this birth the angels proclaim:

Glory to God in the highest heaven,
and on earth peace among those whom he favors! (Luke 2:14)

Zechariah had already announced the visit of the "dawn from on high" or the "rising sun" signifying the messianic age:

By the tender mercy of our God,
    the dawn from on high will break upon us,
to give light to those who sit in darkness and in the shadow of death,
    to guide our feet into the way of peace. (Luke 1:78-79)

Obviously we have to face up to the strange saying of Jesus:

Do not think that I have come to bring peace to the earth; I have
not come to bring peace, but a sword. (Matt 10:34)

This saying provokes surprise, and can even cause spirits to be troubled. It must surely be understood that by pronouncing these words Jesus is in no way trying to bring about a revolt, in the manner of the zealots, but that he is referring to the tension that

[15] Cf. ABD, s.v. "Peace."

the preaching of the kingdom of God necessarily provokes. We may remember the words of the old man Simeon, when Jesus was presented in the Temple as a baby:

> This child is destined for the falling and rising of many in Israel, and to be a sign that will be opposed so that the inner thoughts of many will be revealed.

And he added, addressing Mary, the mother of Jesus:

> And a sword will pierce your own soul too. (Luke 2:34-35)

In the Beatitudes, which can be considered as Jesus's own "manifesto," the importance of peace is emphasized:

> Blessed are the peacemakers, for they will be called children of God. (Matt 5:9)

Jesus himself brings peace, for he says to his apostles:

> Peace I leave with you; my peace I give to you. I do not give to you as the world gives. (John 14:27)

Commenting on this verse, the *Traduction Oecuménique de la Bible* notes that peace is always linked with the person of Christ and with his presence.[16] Jesus himself clarifies matters for his disciples:

> The hour is coming, indeed it has come, when you will be scattered, each one to his home, and you will leave me alone. Yet I am not alone because the Father is with me. I have said this to you, so that in me you may have peace. In the world you face persecution. But take courage, I have conquered the world. (John 16:32-33)

---

[16] Cf. TOB, p. 335, n. *h*.

The Risen Jesus, victor over death, comes to bring peace to his disciples, who have locked themselves in for fear of the Jews:

> Jesus came and stood among them and said, "Peace be with you." After he said this, he showed them his hands and his side. Then the disciples rejoiced when they saw the Lord. Jesus said to them again: "Peace be with you. As the Father has sent me, so I send you." (John 20:19-21)

The disciples are sent to give witness to Christ and to contribute to the coming of the kingdom of God, a kingdom of which peace is an essential characteristic. As Paul writes:

> For the kingdom of God is not food and drink but righteousness and peace and joy in the Holy Spirit. (Rom 14:17)

In fact, peace is recognized as one of the dimensions of the fruit of the Spirit (cf. Gal 5:22).

Paul speaks often of the "God of peace":[17]

> The God of peace be with all of you. Amen. (Rom 15:33)

> Finally, brothers, rejoice. Put things in order, listen to my appeal, agree with one another, live in peace; and the God of love and peace will be with you. (2 Cor 13:11 NRSV with alternative readings)

> Now may the Lord of peace himself give you peace at all times in all ways. (2 Thess 3:16)

Will this God of peace be Himself our recompense? Will God be our inheritance? This is what two letters of the Pauline corpus, Colossians and Ephesians, would suggest.

---

[17] See ABD, s.v. "Peace"; in 2 Thessalonians 3:16 we find the expression "the Lord of Peace."

May you be made strong with all the strength that comes from his [God's] glorious power, and may you be prepared to endure everything with patience, while joyfully giving thanks to the Father, who has enabled you to share in the inheritance of the saints in the light. (Col 1:12)

I pray that the God of our Lord Jesus Christ, the Father of glory, may give you a spirit of wisdom and revelation as you come to know him, so that, with the eyes of your heart enlightened, you may know what is the hope to which he has called you, what are the riches of his glorious inheritance among the saints. (Eph 1:17-18)

We enjoy this inheritance already, but it will only be fully ours when we enter into the fullness of God. The following is the continuation of this passage from Ephesians:

. . . and [and that you may know] what is the immeasurable greatness of his power for us who believe, according to the working of his great power. God put this power to work in Christ when he raised him from the dead and seated him at his right hand in the heavenly places, far above all rule and authority and power and dominion, and above every name that is named, not only in this age but also in the age to come. And he has put all things under his feet and has made him the head of all things for the church, which is his body, the fullness of him who fills all in all. (Eph 1:19-23)

It is good to return also to the letter to the Colossians:

He has rescued us from the power of darkness and transferred us into the kingdom of his beloved Son, in whom we have redemption, the forgiveness of sins. He is the image of the invisible God, the firstborn of all creation; for in him all things in heaven and on earth were created, things visible and invisible, whether thrones or dominions or rulers or powers—all things have been created through him and for him. He himself is before all things, and in him all things hold together. He is the head of the body, the church; he is the beginning, the firstborn from the dead, so that he might come to have first place in everything. For in him all the fullness of God was pleased to dwell, and through him God was pleased to reconcile to himself all things, whether on earth or in heaven, by making peace through the blood of his cross. (Col 1:13-20)

This vision of the end-time should encourage us to continue along the way:

As you therefore have received Christ Jesus the Lord, continue to live your lives, in him, rooted and built up in him and established in the faith, just as you were taught, abounding in thanksgiving. . . . For in him the whole fullness of deity dwells bodily, and you have come to fullness in him, who is the head of every ruler and authority. (Col 2:6-10)

What should be understood here by the term *bodily*? According to the *Traduction Oecuménique de la Bible* the author of the letter is referring to the body of Christ with regard to the person of the risen Lord and to the church; the context shows how divine life is concentrated in Christ but spreads from him to the baptized.[18] It is therefore in and through the risen Christ that God gives of Himself. The resurrection of Jesus remains central to the Christian faith, and this impels Paul to write:

If there is no resurrection of the dead, then Christ has not been raised; and if Christ has not been raised, then our proclamation has been in vain and your faith has been in vain. (1 Cor 15:13-14)

[18] Cf. TOB, p. 609, n. *q*.

This leads Paul to make a clear profession of faith:

> But in fact Christ has been raised from the dead, the first fruits of those who have died. (1 Cor 15:20)

Thus we are led to contemplate what will happen at the end of time:

> Then comes the end, when he [Christ] hands over the kingdom to God the Father, after he has destroyed every ruler and every authority and power. For he must reign until he has put all his enemies under his feet. The last enemy to be destroyed is death. For "God has put all things in subjection under his feet." But when it says "All things are put in subjection," it is plain that this does not include the one who put all things in subjection under him. When all things are subjected to him, then the Son himself will also be subjected to the one who put all things in subjection under him, so that God may be all in all. (1 Cor 15:24-28)

It could be said that there we have the perfect expression of *islâm*. It is the return to the essential mystery of God, where the distinction of Persons does not create plurality and where we ourselves, and all that God has purified according to his will, continue to exist in Him.

This vision gives meaning and direction to all our activity in this world. In our relations, we aim to build up mutual understanding and peace, values of the Kingdom, and an anticipation of that peace which is in God, and which is God.

Beyond our differences, we are conscious of the unity of origin and destiny that we share. The unity that we are aiming for is already anticipated each time there is real contact made in truth, in an atmosphere of respect, so that real if imperfect communion is achieved.

What is required of us is that we be servants of this Kingdom, worthless servants, surely, and we are indeed conscious of this, disinterested servants we would hope to be, so that one day we may hear the Lord saying:

> Well done, good and faithful servant. . . . Come and join in your master's happiness. (Matt 25:21, 23 JB)

We shall find ourselves in the end together with a multitude of brothers and sisters, a great throng made up of all nations, tribes, peoples and languages. And we shall say:

> Amen! Blessing and glory and wisdom
> and thanksgiving and honor
> and power and might
> be to our God forever and ever! Amen. (Rev 7:12)

Conclusion

How should these reflections on the Beautiful Names of God be concluded? Is it really necessary to conclude? Of course, normally we do not spend the whole of our lives in reflection. We are expected, and we expect of ourselves, to pass into action. In the Christian tradition, retreats and spiritual exercises, whether they last thirty days, as in the Spiritual Exercises of St. Ignatius of Loyola, or eight days, or five days, or just over a weekend, aim at having an influence on our daily life. *I'tikâf*, retiring for a time of seclusion, a practice that is known in the Islamic tradition, can aim at the same result. In addressing God by means of His Names, we open ourselves to His will and we prepare ourselves to receive whatever He wishes to give us. After a time of intense prayer, we return to the normal activities of daily life, but with our spirit renewed, and with the desire to live as contemplatives in action. According to this view, we could say that reflection and meditation on the Names of God never come to an end.

It must be admitted also that the meditations proposed in this book have not been able to cover the entire ninety-nine Beautiful Names of God. This was never intended, and it was pointed out right from the beginning that a selection of some of the Names would be made. Nevertheless, more than sixty Names have been mentioned, although some of them only in passing without having been given much attention. This still leaves some thirty or more that have been passed over in silence. Is it true that attention was given exclusively to those Names that a Christian might find truly beautiful, leaving aside some Names that might arouse embarrassment or perplexity? Have those Names for which there do not appear to be any correspondents in the Bible simply been avoided? What answer can be given to this objection?

First of all, it could be pointed out that some very attractive Names have been passed over in silence, Names such as *al-laṭîf*, the Benevolent, *al-ḥalîm*, the Gentle One, or *al-muqît*, the Nourisher. On the other hand, some difficult Names, such as *al-jabbâr*, the Very Strong or the Oppressor, and *al-qahhâr*, the Dominator, which express the power and might of God, have been covered in chapter 5 on "God the King." It is true that *al-muntaqim*, the Avenger, appears nowhere in this book, but this is not because the Name has no equivalent in the Bible. On the contrary, we find in the book of Job the cry of the sufferer: "For I know that my Redeemer lives" (Job 19:25), a triumphant acclamation rendered familiar by the aria of this title in Handel's *Messiah*. This Name "Redeemer" translates the Hebrew term *goel*, the "avenger of blood," the closest relative to the victim of a murder who has the duty of avenging this death, for he must defend the rights and the honor of his relatives.[1] This term is subsequently applied to God, who is the *goel* of the people of Israel,[2] the one who redeems His people, who is their Defender. So we find the following prayer:

[1] Cf. JB on Numbers 35:19, p. 217, n. 35*a*, and on Isaiah 41:14, p. 1027, n. *k*.
[2] Cf. Isaiah 41:14; Jeremiah 50:34.

Let the words of my mouth and the meditation of my heart
  be acceptable to you,
O Lᴏʀᴅ, my rock and my redeemer. (Ps 19:14)

Although the Name of Avenger or Defender does not occur in the NT, the theme of redemption is well and truly present.[3]

We know that Job, after all his protestations of innocence, is reduced to silence before God. We may perhaps have a similar experience. We give praise to the Lord by using His Beautiful Names, but in the end we are not completely satisfied. We come to realize that human words, even if they are inspired, are insufficient; human language is inadequate to express the true nature of God. It is for a good reason that the Islamic tradition reserves the knowledge of the hundredth Name, the Supreme Name of God, to God Himself.[4] After all our expressions of praise, we are inclined to remain silent. This silence, however, does not arise out of embarrassment, or out of fear or shame when faced with the immensity of God. It is rather the silence of the friend who is happy to be in the presence of One he loves and of whose love he is certain. It is, in fact, a silence of fullness to which only God can guide us.

[3] Cf. Mark 10:45 and Romans 3:24 with the note in the JB, p. 273, n. *j.*

[4] On the question of the Supreme Name see Gimaret, *Les noms divins*, pp. 85–94.

Afterword

Archbishop Michael Fitzgerald's book *Praise the Name of the Lord* should be considered a useful contribution to the well-established genre of Islamic theology that deals with the Divine names and attributes, *al-Asmâ' wa-l-Sifât* or *Sifât Allâh*. Among the books in the genre is *Tafsîr Asmâ' Allâh al-Husnâ* by Ibrahim bin Sahel al-Zujjaj (d. 923). Al-Zujjaj, as a philologist, lists ninety-nine names and gives the meaning of each, one by one. Archbishop Fitzgerald not only lists the Divine names but also explains them and how they are presented in the Qur'an while comparing them to the way they are used in the Bible. For example, the Divine names *al-Rahmân*, the Most-Compassionate, and *al-Rahîm*, the Most-Merciful,[1] are the most frequently mentioned of God's names in the Qur'an and they are found in the Islamic formula that begins 113 chapters in the Qur'an: *Bismillâh*

---

[1] As Archbishop Fitzgerald mentioned, the best way to translate *al-Rahman* and *al-Rahim*, not to mention the other names of God, into English is debated. They certainly are both rooted in the root *r.h.m.* which essentially means mercy, and both could be translated as mercy. Without getting into all of the theological debates, I will use my own preferred translations with all due respect given to the archbishop's understanding.

al-Rahmân al-Rahîm, "In the name of God, the Most-Merciful, the Most-Compassionate." The archbishop mentions these Divine names and at the same time relates them to verses from the Bible, especially the psalms and the Gospels. This style shows the similarities between God's names in Islam and the way God is understood in the Christian tradition. Regarding God's mercy, the Gospel of Luke (6:36) says: "Be merciful, just as your Father is merciful."

Archbishop Fitzgerald is careful enough to ensure that his interpretation of the verses from the Qur'an which he discusses is accurate and sensitive to the Islamic reading of the text. I agree with his approach that the Divine names are *tawqîfî*, which means that people cannot name God as they wish. According to Islamic theology, Divine names must be based on the texts, i.e., the Qur'an and the sayings of the Prophet, or compatible with what is mentioned in the texts. God is exalted. This is to avoid naming God with inappropriate names. Furthermore, such a prohibition of non-textually based names eliminates the possibility of vain or malicious names for God. Despite these theological limits and prohibitions, there are Divine names that are not found in the Qur'an. All of this helps us to understand God. All of these names are beautiful. This idea of beautiful names is in the Qur'an: "To God belong the Most-Beautiful Names so call Him by them, and leave those who blaspheme His Names. They will be recompensed for the things that they did" (7:180).

In the invocations of the Prophet of Islam, we find many names of God that are not directly present in the Qur'an. These names and attributes are generally drawn from Divine actions. For example, "The Provider of every creature that is receiving sustenance," "the Helper of those who are abandoned," "the One

Who is the Refuge of all who are oppressed," "the One through Whom all things exist," "the One Who is faithful in His promise," "the One who is subtle in His nearness," or "The One Who is Splendid in His tremendousness." Hundreds of these are found in a prayer of the Prophet, published as a small book called *al-Jaw-shân al-Kabîr*.

Islamic theology gives paramount importance to the attributes and the names of God. Almost all theological manuals have sections and chapters dedicated to discussions of the Divine attributes and names. From the earliest theologians to contemporary scholars and theologians, there is a tremendous literature concerning the names of God. Two of countless examples are a book by al-Bayhaqi (d. 1066) called *Al-Asmâ' wa-l-Sifât*, or *The [Divine] Names and Attributes*, and one by al-Ghazali (d. 1111) called *Sharh Asmâ' Allâh al-Husnâ*, or *Commentary on the Beautiful Names of God*, which deals with the interpretation of the names of God. Other prominent scholars, mystics, and theologians such as Ibn al-Arabi, Rumi, and Said Nursi have written extensively on the meaning and explanation of the Divine names.

Some Muslim theologians divide the attributes of God into two categories. The first group is called *dhâtî*, which means related to the essence of God. These are attributes that are given only to God; no other creature shares these attributes with God. They are known as the six attributes of God, most of which can be derived from Qur'an chapter 112, *Al-Ikhlâs*, as well as other places in the Qur'an. The first is that God is Necessarily Existent (*Wujûd* or *Wâjib al-Wujûd*), i.e., God does not need anything for His existence and God does not have opposites. The second and third are *Qidam* and *Baqâ'*, which are each related to the eternity of God. *Qidam* indicates that God does not have a beginning, and *Baqâ'* means that there is no end for God, as is found in Psalm 90:2, "from everlasting to everlasting you are God." The fourth attribute, *Mukhâlafa li-l-hawâdith*, is related to the concept that God does not resemble anything else. This means that God does not resemble any creature. Muslim theologians have expressed this by saying, "Anything that comes to our mind, God is different from that." The fifth is related to the oneness of God (*Wahdâniyya*). God is One as the Qur'an says: "Say [O Muhammad:] God is only One." The sixth attribute is related to the self-sustainability of the Divine (*Qiyâm bi-nafsi*). This means that God does not need any cause for His existence. Cause and effect are under His control, and there is no cause to help God.

Similar to these exclusive Essence-related attributes of God, there are some attributes related to the essence of God that can be used for both God and human beings. When these attributes are used for God, they are used unlimitedly, while for human beings they are used with limits. These attributes are numbered by Muslim theologians generally as seven. The first attribute is Life (*Hayât*). This means that God is the Living One. God is the source of life. All living creatures take their life from God. The second Divine attribute of this genre is Knowledge (*'ilm*). That is, God knows everything: the things that happen in the present, past, and future. Nothing can be hidden from God. Human beings also know, but their knowledge is limited. In fact, the things that they do not know are much greater than the things that they do know. The third attribute of God is Hearing (*Sam'*). That is, God hears everything, whether said in secret or in the open. Even a soft whisper is known by God. Even if a person speaks inside himself or herself, God hears it. Muslim theologians would say, "God hears the sound of the feet of an ant walking in a dark night

on a rock." The fourth attribute in this genre is Seeing (*Basar*).
God sees everything. Nothing can be hidden from God's sight.
The fifth is God is Willing (*Irâda*). That is to say, what God wills
happens as He wishes. There are no obstacles for the will of God.
He does what He wants as He wants. Sixth is Power (*Qudra*). God
has an unlimited power. For God, to spin our planet is as easy
as to spin a top. The seventh attribute of God in this category is
Speaking (*Kalâm*). That is, God speaks and has the power of all
tongues.

There is a third category of the Divine names related to the
actions of God. For example, God is the Opener of seeds. God
is the Changer of hearts. God is the Knower of the seen and the
unseen. God is the Most Merciful of those who are merciful. The
Divine attributes and names that are related to the actions of God
are unlimited. Indicating the importance of these Divine names,
the Prophet says "God has ninety-nine names; the one who memo-
rizes [or counts] them will enter Paradise." The commentators of
the hadith would say that merely counting or memorizing them is
not meant, otherwise entering Paradise would be easy and cheap.
What is meant is to contemplate the Divine names and through
this contemplation to grasp the meaning of the Names. It has to be
noted that understanding the essence of God is beyond the capacity
of human beings. Therefore, it has been narrated that the Prophet
said not to contemplate the essence of God but to contemplate
the art of God. "Contemplating the essence of God will lead you
astray." Contemplating the art of God is in fact contemplating the
reflections of the Divine names. Therefore, one can understand
the Divine names and through the Divine names, one can have
an understanding of God. Human beings have been given limited
attributes in order to learn the unlimited attributes of God. For ex-

ample, human beings have power, but that power is limited. This limited power gives human beings a sense of what power means and hence an understanding of the nature of the unlimited power of God. Without this power, human beings would not be able to recognize the power of God. Therefore, human beings are led to the Divine name *al-Qâdir*, the Most-Powerful. Knowledge, will, etc. are all comparable to this Divine power. If human beings see a remarkable cleanliness in the universe, especially in this planet, when rain comes and cleans and beautiful green trees and grass sprout and cover the face of the earth like a carpet, if human beings have not touched it, it is clean. Such cleanliness leads human beings to the Divine name *al-Quddûs*. Therefore, the entirety of the cleanliness on the face of the earth, in which millions of workers, animals, insects, and microbes, etc. are constantly involved, is a reflection of this Divine name. In other words, by this Divine name human beings understand God. The visible world is a reflection of the Divine names. If we need to make an analogy, it would be comparable with the painting of a famous artist, like Picasso. So when one looks at a painting by Picasso, he or she will see physical elements in it: ink, paint, brushstrokes, the canvas. But when the painting is seen in an encompassing way, one can see the ideas in it: the consciousness of the artist, the hands of the artist, the skill of the artist, the skill of balancing, etc. Many attributes of the painter can be seen in the painting. Therefore, a flower is a Divine painting showing the attributes of God and displaying His magnificence. Similarly an atom and the sun, all elements of the universe, are all Divine paintings.

The concept of the Divine names and their reflections on human beings, the planet, and the universe is an essential element of Islamic theology. The more one reflects on the Divine names, the more one is elevated in the realm of spirituality. A reflecting human being becomes a mirror for the Divine names. The human being that becomes such a mirror becomes a perfect human being. This human being empowers his or her own relationship with the Divine as well as his or her relationship with fellow human beings.

This brings us to a major theme of the book: encouraging dialogue. Dialogue between the two largest religions, Christianity and Islam, is a global necessity. *Praise the Name of the Lord* surely is a point of dialogue between Christians and Muslims, and perhaps this is what the archbishop is aiming at. Moreover, through the incorporation of the Hebrew Bible, I would argue that Jews are included as well. Under one name the author refers to the Qur'an, which is his essential source, but he also refers to the Hebrew Bible and the Gospels. I would argue that this is entirely compatible with the overall Qur'anic approach, because the Qur'an refers to the Torah, the Psalms, and to the Gospels, in various verses. Occasionally it says "We have written . . ." For example, a verse refers to the Psalms saying, "Surely We have written in the Psalms [*Zabûr*], after the Torah, that my wholesome servants will inherit the earth" (Q 21:105). Similarly, the Qur'an refers to the Torah, especially about the punishment of criminals when it says, "Surely we have sent down the Torah . . . and We have written in it a life for a life, an eye for an eye, a tooth for a tooth, an equal wound for a wound" (Q 5:44-5). These verses and others show that the Torah, the Psalms, and the Gospels were earlier messages of God for humanity, and the fact that they and the Qur'an share the same message of God is an important element of dialogue. Therefore, it is Qur'anic methodology to make connection between the Qur'an and earlier Divine revelations, to see a common ground between adherents of the religions of the Abrahamic family.

This book is important for Muslims to see that despite many layers of translations, still the earlier Divine books contain similar qualities and attributes of God as those referred to in the Qur'an. Archbishop Fitzgerald successfully makes this possible through comparison. This book is also useful for Christians and Jews since it gives considerable details of the Divine names in the Qur'an in a way that is accessible for those with little previous knowledge of Islam. Therefore, one can find many topics in the book that any interfaith dialogue group with members from the Abrahamic traditions can find useful. The archbishop rightly refers to an organization of interfaith dialogue in France known as the Christian-Muslim Research Group. This group has been in dialogue since 1977. I can testify from my own experience that in the United States and the rest of the world, dialogues between members of different faiths have been enriching, positive, and fruitful. In the city where I live, I am in contact with a group of people who meet every three weeks to discuss the Bible and the Qur'an. The group is called the "Qur'an and Bible Study Group." Hence, this book can serve as a good reference for these types of groups that are practicing interfaith dialogue.

Considering the Divine names that are discussed in the book, in a comparative way, the book provides a remarkable ground and a rich resource for those who would like to know God's names in Islam, and more specifically to know God, which in Islamic theology is considered the highest goal of the realm of creation.

Zeki Saritoprak
John Carroll University
Cleveland Heights, Ohio

The Most Beautiful Names of God

In the Name of God, the Lord of Mercy, the Giver of Mercy.[1]

The Most Excellent Names belong to God: use them to call on Him.

He is God—there is no divinity except Him.

The Lord of Mercy, the Giver of Mercy,

the King, the Holy One, the Source of Peace, the Granter of Security, the Guardian,

the Almighty, the Compeller, the Truly Great (the Haughty), the Creator, the Originator, the Shaper (the Organizer), the Most Forgiving (the Pardoner),

the All Powerful (the Dominator), the Ever Giving, the Provider (the Dispenser of all good), the Judge (the Victorious Revealer), the All Knowing, the Withholder, the Expander,

[1] The list of Names of God was most probably compiled by Walîd b. Muslim al-Dimashqî (d. 195/810) on the basis of a tradition going back to Abû Hurayra, a companion of Muhammad. It is found in the collection of *hadîths* made by al-Tirmidhî (d. 279/892). Three sources have been drawn on for the English translation of the Names: *The Qur'an*, trans. M. A. S. Abdel Haleem (Oxford: Oxford University Press, 2010); Louis Gardet, s.v. "Al-Asma' al-Husna," in EI[2]; Gerhard Böwering, "God and His Attributes," in EQ. The translation follows, line by line, the original disposition of the Arabic text.

the One who brings low, the One who raises high, the One who honors, the One who abases, the All Hearing, the All Seeing, the Judge, the Just,

the All Subtle (the Benevolent), the All Aware (the Sagacious), the Most Forbearing (the Gentle), the Tremendous (the Inaccessible), the Most Forgiving (the Very Indulgent), the Most Appreciative (the Very Grateful), the Most High, the Most Great (the Great),

the Watchful (the Vigilant), the Controller (the Nourisher), the One who keeps account of everything (the Reckoner), the Majestic, the Generous, the Watcher (the Jealous Guardian), the One who is ready to answer (the Assenter), the All Pervading (the Omnipresent),

the All Wise (the Wise), the Most Loving (the Very Loving), the Glorious, the Revivifier, the Witness, the Truth (the Real), the Protector (the Trustee), the Strong,

the Ever Mighty (the Unshakable), the Protector (the Friend), the One Worthy of All Praise, The One who takes Account (the Numberer), the Innovator, the One who brings about the Return, the Creator of Life, the Creator of Death,

the Ever Living (the Living), the Ever Watchful (the Self-Subsisting), the Opulent (the Perfect), the Noble, the One (the Unique), the Eternal (the Impenetrable), the Powerful, the All Powerful,

the One who brings Near, the One who sends Away (the Repriever), the First, the Last, the Manifest (the Patent), the Hidden (the Latent), the Protector (the Reigning), the Most High (the Exalted),

the One who causes Piety, the Ever Relenting (the Repentant), the Avenger, the Pardoner, the Most Compassionate, the Holder of all Control (the Master of the Kingdom),

Full of Majesty and Bestowing Honor (the Possessor of Majesty and Generosity), the Equitable (the Just), the Gatherer (the Assembler), the Self-Sufficient (the Independent), the Enricher, the Defender,

the Afflicter, the One who favors, the Light, the Guide, the Originator
(the Creator-Inventor),

the Enduring (the Eternal), the Inheritor, the Leader, the Very Patient.

May His majesty be magnified, and may His Names be declared holy.

My God, indeed I am Your servant, the son of Your servant, the son
of Your handmaid. My forelock is in Your hands: Your judgment concerning me is decisive and Your decree is just. I therefore beseech You,
by each one of the Names that belongs to You, which You have chosen
for Yourself, or which You have revealed in Your book, or which You
have taught to one of Your creatures, or the usage of which You have
reserved to Yourself according to the knowledge You have of Your own
Mystery, to render the glorious Qur'an true nourishment for my heart
and light for my vision; may it dispel in me all sadness and remove from
me every worry and affliction. Amen!

Bibliography

Abd el-Jalîl, Jean-Mohammed. *Aspects intérieurs de l'Islam*. Paris: Le Seuil, 1949.

Abdel Haleem, M. A. S. *The Qur'an*. Oxford: Oxford University Press, 2010.

The Anchor Bible Dictionary. New York: Doubleday, 1992.

Benedict XVI. *Spe Salvi* [Encyclical Letter Saved in Hope]. http://w2 .vatican.va/content/benedict-xvi/en/encyclicals/documents/hf _ben-xvi_enc_20071130_spe-salvi.html.

Bidar, Abdennour. *L'islam sans soumission. Pour un existentialisme musulman*. Paris: Albin Michel, 2008.

Caspar, Robert. *A Historical Introduction to Islamic Theology. Muhammad and the Classical Period*. Rome: PISAI, 1998.

Cragg, Kenneth. *Alive to God: Muslim and Christian Prayer*. Oxford: Oxford University Press, 1970.

Eliade, Mircea. *Patterns in Comparative Religion*. London: Sheed and Ward, 1958.

Etchegaray, Roger. *J'avance comme un âne: petits clins d'oeil au Ciel et à la terre*. Paris: Fayard, 1984.

Gaudeul, J. M. *Encounters and Clashes: Islam and Christianity in History*. Vol. 1: *A Survey*. Vol. 2: *Texts*. Rome: Pontifical Institute of Arabic and Islamic Studies, 2000.

al-Ghazâlî. *The Ninety-Nine Beautiful Names of God* (*al-maqṣad al-asnâ fî sharḥ asmâ' Allâh al-ḥusnâ*). Translated with notes by David B. Burrell and Nazih Daher. Cambridge, UK: The Islamic Texts Society, 1992.

Gimaret, Daniel. *Les noms divins en Islam*. Paris: Les Editions du Cerf, 1988.

Gioia, Francesco. *Interreligious Dialogue: The Official Teaching of the Catholic Church from the Second Vatican Council to John Paul II (1963–2005)*. Boston: Pauline Books & Media, 2006.

Lalljee, Yousuf N. *Know Your Islam*. 2nd edition. Bombay: Anjuman-e-Himayatul Islam, 1970.

Leon-Dufour, Xavier. *Vocabulaire de Théologie Biblique*. Paris: Les Editions du Cerf, 1964.

Moloney Francis J. *The Gospel of John*. Sacra Pagina, Collegeville, MN: Liturgical Press, 1998.

Muslim-Christian Research Group. *The Challenge of the Scriptures: The Bible and the Qur'an*. Maryknoll, NY: Orbis Books, 1989.

Scarabel, Angelo. *Preghiera sui Nomi più belli. I novantanove Nomi di Dio nella tradizione islamica*. Genoa: Marietti, 1996.

Sells, Michael. *Approaching the Qur'an*. 2nd edition. Ashland, OR: White Cloud Press, 2007².

Yusuf Ali, Abdullah. *The Holy Qur'an*. Beirut: Dar al Arabia, 1968.